Natchez

An Illustrated History

Natchez

An Illustrated History

by
David G. Sansing, Sim C. Callon
and Carolyn Vance Smith

PLANTATION PUBLISHING COMPANY
Natchez, Mississippi

ISBN 0-9631823-1-5
FIRST EDITION

Copyright 1992 by the
PLANTATION PUBLISHING COMPANY
P. O. Box 17842
Natchez, MS 39122-7842

Copies of this publication may be obtained by
sending check or money order to the address
above. Cost: $14.95 plus $2.00 for shipping
and handling. Make payment to Plantation
Publishing Company.

Contents

The Mississippi River near Natchez

Chapter 1

In the Valley
of the Sun Kings

For aeons the lush alluvial valleys of the lower Mississippi River nourished an environment so serene and sylvan that early European explorers compared it to the biblical Eden. And for several centuries before the sound of Spanish arms broke the Southern stillness, that pristine wilderness had nurtured a native American culture of remarkable achievement. A sun-worshipping tribe who called their chief the "Sun King" or "Great Sun" was living in nine villages scattered along the banks of St. Catherine's Creek when Sieur de La Salle first encountered them in 1682. That tribe, later identified as the Sunset Indians but now known as the Natchez Indians, is believed by some scholars to be the last surviving remnant of an earlier and more advanced group called the Mississippian Culture.

The sudden flowering of this culture, a pre-Columbian civilization which one anthropologist has described as a "cultural explosion," began around A.D. 1000. It climaxed at about the time or perhaps just before the European settlement. This civilization never developed a written language and left no historical or written records. The enticing bits of information that are known about the Mississippian Culture have been compiled by archaeologists and anthropologists through the skillful interpretation of artifacts and other archaeological evidence. It is believed that the cultural achievements of the Mississippian period may have been sparked by some contact with the more advanced Indian societies of Mexico.

The Mississippian Culture was widely dispersed throughout the Southeast and reached into the heartland

LaSalle at the mouth of the Mississippi River, about 1682

of North America along both the east and west banks of the Mississippi River, which the Indians called the "Father of Waters." The people of that period developed an extensive horticulture which incorporated maize, beans, squash, melons and a great variety of other indigenous plants. Because they were successful agriculturalists, the Mississippian Culture achieved a population density unmatched by their more primitive predecessors. They lived in large towns of 100 acres or more as well as in smaller hamlets of 10 to 20 acres. Their villages were built beside an oxbow lake or alongside a creek in the riverine areas where there was good, sandy loam.

Examples of pictography, which substituted for a written language of the Mississippi Indians

Most of the large towns and even some of the smaller villages were palisaded, an indication perhaps that organized and large-scale aggression was an unfortunate feature of that pristine society. The larger towns employed a mound complex which consisted of several small mounds on which tribal officials lived and at least one large mound for religious and ceremonial purposes. The ceramics produced by the Mississippian people were highly decorative and included molded images of both human and animal figures.

The people of the Mississippian Culture traded extensively in hematite, steatite, galena, sea shells, mica, fresh water pearls, quartz crystals and other exotic items. Over those trade routes also spread an elaborate set of rituals and religious practices called the Southern Ceremonial Complex, or the Southern Cult. One interesting feature of that primitive belief system was the use of an intricate configuration of natural and abstract symbols which included a reversed swastika, dancing winged human figures, winged serpents, birds of prey, snakes and spiders. Also very prominent in the religious symbolism were the sun and large ceremonial mounds. Two of the largest of those are Cahokia Mound near St. Louis and Emerald Mound near Natchez.

Because the Natchez Indians continued to use mounds and other ceremonial structures, and especially because their theocratic caste system was quite different from the social organization of other Southeastern woodland Indians, they are considered to be the last relic of the Mississippian Culture. Oral traditions among the Natchez recalled an ancient epoch of Natchez history when the tribe numbered 200,000 and was ruled by 1,900 "suns" or chieftains. The domain of that tribe of former glory extended from the Natchez region up to the confluence of the Mississippi and the Ohio Rivers. Although anthropologists discount the possibility, the Natchez themselves believed that they had migrated into the Lower Mississippi Valley from Mexico and that they were descendants of the Aztecs. La Page du Pratz, a French chronicler who lived among the Natchez, reported that the Temple Guardian told him stories of invaders who carried magic sticks that spewed fire and death, perhaps a primitive remembrance of either Cortes and the conquistadors who marched across Mexico in 1519 or of Hernando DeSoto and his expedition in 1542.

The first contact between Europeans and the Natchez Indians may have occurred during De Soto's expedition.

Road sign marking the historic St. Catherine Creek, which winds throughout Adams County

St. Catherine Creek in modern times, flowing toward the Mississippi River

Emerald Mound, built by ancestors of the Natchez about A.D. 1400, the second largest ceremonial mound in the United States, covering nearly 8 acres

Chief Quigaltanqui, whose relentless pursuit of the Spanish invaders was described by the chroniclers of De Soto's expedition, was probably a Natchez, although he was not identified as such. The word Natchez, the meaning of which is not known, first appeared in La Salle's narratives of 1682.

At the time of European discovery, the Natchez numbered approximately 3,500, which included 1,000 warriors. The tribe lived in nine villages scattered along St. Catherine's Creek, near the present city of Natchez. The main village of the Natchez, where the Great Sun lived, was known as the Grand Village. It was considered sacred by members of the tribe. Also important was White Apple Village, a few miles south of the Grand

Village. According to Andre Penicaut, another French chronicler who lived among the Natchez in the summer of 1704, the Natchez were "the most courteous and civil [Indians] along the banks of the Missicipy." Penicaut left a description of their pristine setting:

> The Village of the Natchez is the most beautiful that could be found in Louisiana. It is beautified by very pretty walks which nature, and not artifice, has formed there. Around it are flower-adorned prairies, broken by little hills upon which there are thickets of all kinds of fragrant trees. Several little streams of very clear water issue from beneath a mountain visible for two leagues across the prairies and, after watering them in many places, they gather up into two big creeks which encircle the village, beyond which they unite in the form of a small river which flows over very fine gravel and passes on...into the Missicipy. The water in it is very pleasant to drink, being cold as ice in summer and tepid in winter.

Penicaut also described the bounty of that unspoiled wilderness with breathless wonder. In their villages, he wrote, "one finds every amenity. All the necessaries of life are here, such as buffaloes, cows, [deer], chickens and turkeys and an abundance of geese. There are also fish in abundance; all kinds of them; there are carp weighing more than 20 pounds, which are of an exquisite taste. As for fruit there is more than any other place in Louisiana. They have many cherries, which grow in bunches like our grapes in France [and] are excellent in brandy. In the woods everywhere," he continued, "are many peach trees, plum trees, mulberry trees and walnuts. They have three kinds of walnut trees: there are some that bear nuts as big as one's fist [but] the best are scarcely bigger than one's thumb; these they call pacanes."

The bounty of that generous land produced tall and robust warriors, many of whom were more than 6 feet tall. Penicaut and other French chroniclers described the Natchez men as very handsome, with a "proud air." And even by European standards the women were also

Above, a hunting scene as drawn by an early European explorer showing elaborate animal disguises for the hunters, and, right, a Natchez Indian depicted by Natchez artist Ruth Latham

attractive, with soft and melodious voices, "as with the singing of birds."

The Natchez language, although it is technically considered a member of the Muskogean language family, was very different from the language spoken by other Muskogean tribes. Two other small nearby tribes, the Taensas and Avoyel, spoke a similar dialect, and, like the Natchez, also practiced voluntary human sacrifice, a tradition that distinguished them and the Natchez from other native American cultures.

The Natchez Tribe was a matrilineal society, with lineage, status and position traced through the female line. The social structure consisted of four distinct groups or classes. The Sun class, or royal family, was the highest order; only from this class were the Great Suns selected. The next two orders, the Nobles and the Honored People, formed the lesser aristocracy. The fourth order, the common class, was identified by a

French word that is translated into English as "Stinkards." The upper classes dressed differently from the Stinkards and also spoke a slightly different dialect.

Anthropologists are not certain, and they do not even agree among themselves, about precisely how the Natchez social system operated. But it is known that members of each class married down into the next lower order. Since there was no class below the common class, they married into the Sun class. Tribal traditions, however, prohibited the offspring of a Stinkard from ever becoming a chief. Only sons of women born to the Sun class could become a Great Sun.

The Great Sun ruled the Natchez as an absolute monarch. His subjects were not allowed to touch him and had to remain at least four feet away when addressing him. His sister, rather than his wife, was accorded the highest honor and status among the female members of the tribe. Also, the Great Sun's first nephew rather than his first son, was the heir to the throne. When a Sun King or some other esteemed member of the tribe died, it was customary for children, warriors and close relatives of the deceased to be sacrificed [normally by strangulation] to accompany the departed soul along the mysterious path into the afterlife. If the Great Sun's wet nurse

A Natchez Indian chief, center, with Choctaw warriors and children, as depicted by A. DeBatz, an early visitor

was still alive upon his death, she also had to be put to death. Parents in the Stinkard class who volunteered their children for the sacrifice became eligible to move up in the social hierarchy. After several years of persuasion by the French Catholic missionaries who lived among them, the Natchez eventually abandoned the practice of human sacrifice.

The Natchez lived in wood-framed huts with thatched roofs. The most dominant and most important structure among the Natchez was a 30-foot high sacred temple which was located in the Grand Village. Inside the temple a fire was kept continuously burning by four warriors who guarded the temple and maintained the fire. If they allowed the fire to go out, they were put to death. The perpetual fire represented the sun, the highest deity in the Natchez pantheon.

The Natchez calendar consisted of 13 moon months, with each year beginning in March. All important council meetings, either among the Natchez chieftains themselves, with other Indian nations or with Europeans, were opened with the smoking of the calumet, or the peace pipe. The importance of this custom was first observed by a French traveler who wrote: "We stayed in their village three days—as long as their calumet lasted." So binding was the tradition of the calumet that many Indian affairs were limited to three days, the normal period of time of a calumet.

As far as the physical appearance of Natchez tribal members, both men and women employed cosmetics to alter their looks, and children of both sexes were kept for long periods of time in specially designed cradles to flatten their heads. Men were clean shaven and heavily tattooed. Both men and women blackened their teeth by daily applications of tobacco and wood ashes. Both sexes also wore clothing from the waist down, but women

Indian temple of the type built by the Natchez, showing cane mats used as shingles and siding

*An Indian
in winter dress*

did not normally cover their bodies from the waist up except in winter. The Natchez had not developed the art of weaving and wore only animal skins or a covering which they fashioned from mulberry bark.

Love, courtship and marriage among the Natchez were a source of consternation to Catholic missionaries and a source of fascination to early French chroniclers. Courtship rituals centered on a dance festival which took place in the public square of the village. Men and women, as well as boys and girls, participated in the ceremonial dance which began at sunset and was accompanied by small drums and the chants of spectators. The village plaza was illuminated by the burning of huge pine knots. At this festival and at other social and recreational events, the Natchez freely imbibed an intoxicant which they made from the fruit of the yaupon bush. Married men did not dance with the young girls, and young boys did not dance with the women. Penicaut described the dance as a form similar to that of "the new cotillion in France."

Lower Mississippi River Valley Indians as depicted by early European visitors

16

Dance générale.

An outdoor dance performed by the Natchez Indians, with men forming the exterior ring and women forming the interior ring

At about midnight during the festival, the elders retired to their huts. The young dancers continued until daylight. After the adults had retired, boys and girls were permitted by tribal traditions to engage in free love. Penicaut described that practice with both disbelief and astonishment. "When a boy has danced with a girl at his side," he wrote in 1704, "he is permitted to escort her beyond the village and into one of the thickets out on the prairie, where he dances with her another cotillion a la Missicipyene." If a child was born of one of those nighttime trysts, the mother was given the choice of keeping and raising the child or of having it put to death, "without the slightest stir," according to Penicaut.

Young Natchez women were allowed to sell or trade their sexual favors for items of value, and by that means they accumulated a worthy dowry which made them more desirable as prospective brides. Although chastity before marriage was not required by the social mores of the Natchez, fidelity after marriage was. Adultery among married women was severely punished, often by death. Marriages, which were normally accompanied by elaborate ceremonies and celebration, were economic and political alliances between two families rather than a romantic union between two individuals. Divorce, or more accurately the discontinuation of a marital arrangement, was easily obtained by the male and required only the agreement between the two families involved.

After the French established a provincial outpost among the Natchez in 1713, and especially after the construction of Fort Rosalie in 1716, the French population steadily increased, and intermarriage with the Natchez became increasingly common. Sexual exploitation of Natchez women by French provincials eventually became a source of deep resentment among Natchez warriors and other tribesmen.

Though the origins of the Natchez are lost in the misty era of prehistory, their demise is well documented. In 1729 Sieur de Chepart, commandant of the French provincial outpost at Fort Rosalie and a hard-drinking

18

Fort Rosalie in the early 1700s

Fort Rosalie and surrounding ravines in the late 1700s

Natchez Indians' Calumet

Marche du Calumet de Paix.

Though the Natchez Indian tribe attacked Fort Rosalie in 1729, killing numerous Frenchmen and seriously damaging the fort, they were also known as peace-loving people. Indeed, all important council meetings of Natchez chieftains, whether with other Indian nations or with Europeans, opened with the smoking of the calumet, or the peace pipe. The importance of this custom was so binding that many Indian affairs were limited to three days, the normal period of time of a calumet.

tobacco planter, decided to enrich himself and enlarge his own land holdings. He demanded tribute from the Natchez and threatened to remove the Great Sun from office. He also threatened to take over one of the tribe's main villages. Records are not clear if he wanted to occupy the Grand Village or the White Apple Village. According to legend, the Great Sun asked for a delay of two moons. He then called a council of chiefs of neighboring tribes to coordinate a strike against the hated invaders. The date of the strike was set, and each chief was given a bundle of sticks to mark the time, one stick being removed from the pile for each day that passed.

When there were no more sticks, the battle was to begin.

According to one of several legends that tell of the destruction of the Natchez nation, the Great Sun in 1729 was the son of a Natchez woman and a French provincial. The mother of the Great Sun had not been admitted to the council when the attack was planned, but she prevailed upon her son to divulge the secret plans to her. She in turn informed the French commandant, who ignored the warning. To save the French garrison, the mother of the Great Sun removed two sticks from his bundle, causing the Natchez warriors to begin their campaign early—without help from allied tribes.

Another legend tells of Stelona, a Natchez princess who was enamored of a French officer. To save her lover, she secretly removed several sticks from the pile, and the attack began early. Some allies of the Natchez, thinking they had struck early to enrich themselves, either did not join the campaign or allied themselves with the French to punish the Natchez. But several other small nearby tribes did join the battle against the French.

With or without allies, the Natchez attacked Fort Rosalie on November 28, 1729, driving the French garrison from the outpost. During the attack the fort was badly damaged, and approximately 250 whites were killed. Many captives were taken, and African slaves held by the French were freed.

Though the Natchez defeated the military garrison at Fort Rosalie, this was not a final blow to French provincialism. It was, instead, a prelude to the destruction of the Natchez nation.

From 1730 to 1732, Louisiana Gov. Sieur de la Perier dispatched a combined force of French soldiers and Choctaw warriors to recapture Fort Rosalie and to punish the Natchez tribe. Many Natchez Indians were killed or sold into slavery during this French military campaign.

Although the Natchez had lost its tribal identity by the mid-1730s, remnants of the tribe remained in the Natchez area for many years. A small band of Natchez,

An artist's conception of the Natchez Indians' attack of Fort Rosalie in 1729

who had managed to escape the French retribution during a severe thunderstorm, found refuge among the Chickasaws in Northeast Mississippi. Some of them made their way into Cherokee country. A few descendants of this small band were later found among the Cherokee in the Oklahoma Territory, still speaking the Natchez language as recently as 1928.

The Natchez tribe was one of the most interesting and unusual and certainly one of the most complex of all native American societies. Tribesmen continue to be studied by anthropologists and have been immortalized by Francois Rene de Chateaubriand in two romantic novels entitled Atala and Rene, which were later combined and published as Les Natchez. This once proud tribe is no more, and America is diminished by its demise.

Chapter 2

In Search of God, Gold and Glory

At various times during the Great Age of Colonization, England, France and Spain all laid claim to the Lower Mississippi Valley, and the Natchez outpost was often the focal point of those rival claims. Thus the early history of Natchez is part of a much larger and more important story, the story of empires won and lost in the Southern wilderness.

From their bases in the Caribbean, Spanish conquistadors, whose motto was "God, Gold and Glory" -- but not necessarily in that order—launched several expeditions onto the American mainland. In 1513 Ponce de Leon discovered Florida, and in 1519 Alonzo de Pineda explored the Mississippi Gulf Coast. Pineda's voyage increased Spanish interest in the Gulf region, with Panfilo de Narvaez making another expedition along the coast in 1528.

The most important early Spanish incursion into the southeastern part of the United States was led by Hernando De Soto. A conquistador who had already won fame and fortune during the Spanish conquest of Peru, De Soto was granted a charter to colonize Florida in 1536. After spending much time and care in assembling an expeditionary force of more than 600 men and women, he landed at Tampa Bay in May 1539. De Soto's expedition also included 200 horses, a drove of swine, a herd of cattle and a pack of dogs. His conquistadors wore coats of mail which made them virtually invincible to the Indians' primitive instruments of warfare. De Soto's goal was to find North America's El Dorados, the cities of riches like those found in South and Central America.

De Soto entered Northeast Mississippi in December 1540 and continued westward until his winter encampment. In the spring of 1541 De Soto broke camp and set out again on his western march. During the first week of May 1541, De Soto and his expedition crossed the Mississippi River approximately 200 miles north of Natchez. After several months De Soto became discouraged at his failure to find the cities of gold. Although archaeologists are not certain of his route, it is believed that he returned to the Mississippi River somewhere north of Natchez. It was there that De Soto died in May 1542 from a long-festering wound suffered in an earlier battle. De Soto was buried in the turbid waters of the great river that will forever be associated with his name. His weary and leaderless band of Spaniards, who numbered less than half of the original expedition, built a crude fleet of flatboats and rafted down the Mississippi to the Gulf Coast, where they were eventually rescued.

After De Soto's expedition left Mississippi soil, the Southeastern woodlands were undisturbed for another 130 years. But the peace of that country had been breached. Squirrels, deer, bear, bison and Indian braves had heard the sound of gunfire. Indians had grown ill and died of white men's diseases for which they had no natural resistance or medicine to cure. The terror and mystery of those invaders sparked among Southeastern Indians a religious awakening and cultural renaissance known as the "Death Cult" or "Buzzard Cult."

LaSalle at the mouth of the Mississippi River, 1682

Little is known about the brief flowering of culture or the drastic decline in the Indian population between De Soto's time and the arrival of the French in the 1670s. But anthropologists estimate that the Indian population in Mississippi declined by as much as 80 percent during the 130 years between De Soto's departure and the coming of La Salle.

The reactivation of European interest in the Natchez region resulted from Indian stories about a long river that "lost itself in the great sea." Gov. Louis Frontenac of French Canada, who was seeking a water route across

Hernando de Soto, a Spanish explorer who in 1541 entered what is now North Mississippi

the North American continent, was encouraged sufficiently by those stories to send Father Jacques Marquette and Louis Joliet to explore the long river. When their expedition reached an unnamed river which is now known as the Arkansas in July 1673, they realized that they were on the River of De Soto, which was well-known to them. Marquette and Joliet then returned to Canada.

French interest in the Mississippi Valley continued, however, and another expedition was conducted in 1682 under Rene Robert Cavalier, Sieur de La Salle. On that initial expedition La Salle made contact with the Natchez Indians, spent some time among them and established friendly relations with them. On April 9, 1682, La Salle finally reached the mouth of the Mississippi. To celebrate that momentous occasion, La Salle held a formal and elaborate ceremony. His men put on fresh uniforms

Sieur d'Iberville, founder of the Louisiana colony, who visited the Natchez Indians in 1700

and lined up with their muskets in hand. After singing several French songs, they fired their muskets while shouting, "Long live the king." La Salle then planted the flag of France in Southern soil and in a loud voice claimed all the lands and tributaries of that mighty river for France. He named the new possession "Louisiana" in honor of Louis XIV, the Sun King of France.

In January 1699, a French expeditionary force under Pierre Le Moyne, Sieur d'Iberville, landed on the Mississippi Gulf Coast. A Canadian-born naval officer and member of a famous French military family, Iberville was sent to Louisiana to defend the new province from Spanish and English incursion and to protect French trade along the Mississippi, a river which linked the French provinces in Illinois and Canada to the Gulf of Mexico.

In 1700 Iberville visited the Natchez village but eventually decided not to build a fort nearby. He did, however, leave a missionary with the Natchez, a Catholic priest, who remained until 1706. The establishment of the Louisiana Province greatly increased trade along the Mississippi River, with contact between the Natchez and the French increasing correspondingly. English traders had also made contact with the Natchez, and after 1708 British agents were frequent visitors to the Natchez region.

As the population of Louisiana increased, intermarriage between French settlers and Indian women also increased. Intermarriage, however, was discouraged by French officials and resented by tribal leaders. In an effort to resolve that growing problem and to attract more French women to Louisiana, colonial authorities initiated a program of mail-order brides.

In 1704, 20 young French girls were brought to the province to be married to the soldiers and settlers in French Louisiana. Within a short time, all but one had married. Because the girls did not adjust very well to the frontier conditions, in 1706 they vowed to leave their husbands and return to France. This "petticoat insurrection," as it was called, did not succeed because French sea captains refused the girls' passage back to France. Over the next several years, perhaps as many as 500 young women, known as "filles a' la casquette," were brought to the Louisiana Province. Each of the girls was given a casquette, or small suitcase, containing a wedding dress and other personal articles. The girls normally came from orphanages, brothels and prisons, but in some cases they were sold by their parents. The casquette girls were under the care of Ursuline nuns until suitable marriage arrangements could be made.

With people settling down, in 1714 Antoine de la Mothe, Sieur de Cadillac, the new governor of Louisiana, established a trading post at the Mississippi River landing below the Natchez bluff. Two years later he directed Jean Baptiste Le Moyne, Sieur d'Bienville, the younger brother of Iberville, to build a fort among the Natchez

Sieur de Bienville, brother of Sieur d'Iberville and a trader with the Natchez Indians in the early 1700s

and to station a small garrison there. Not only was there a need for a way station between the Illinois country and Louisiana but there was also a need for a military presence among the Natchez to prevent them from interrupting French commerce on the Mississippi, as they had done in 1714 when they killed four traders. The Natchez claimed that the hostility between them and the French was caused by Gov. Cadillac's refusal to take the calumet on a visit in 1714. After the construction of Fort Rosalie, which was named in honor of the wife of the Minister of Marine, le Comte de Pontchartrain, several land concessions were granted and French settlers flowed into the area. Fort Rosalie and its environs soon became a flourishing part of the Louisiana Province.

In 1717 John Law, a one-time Scottish gambler who was appointed French Minister of Finance, united the Company of the Indies and the Royal Bank of France.

Thousands of shares were sold in the new joint stock company, which was awarded the proprietorship of the Louisiana Province. The new company published exaggerated accounts of the profit potential of faraway Louisiana with its "fertile soil, balmy air and golden sands." Stock prices skyrocketed, and many Frenchmen liquidated other assets to invest in what became known as the "Mississippi Bubble."

Due largely to the company's aggressive advertising campaign, the population of Louisiana increased dramatically and the Province was subdivided into nine districts. One of the subdivisions was the Natchez District, with Fort Rosalie as headquarters. The population of the Natchez District increased from 303 (of which 111 were slaves) in 1723 to 713 (with 280 slaves) in 1727. Some consideration was given to making Natchez the capital of Louisiana, but New Orleans was eventually selected.

While the Natchez region was under the control of the Company of the Indies, large numbers of African slaves

John Law, whose Company of the Indies acquired Louisiana in 1717 and who in 1723 designated Fort Rosalie as headquarters of the Natchez District

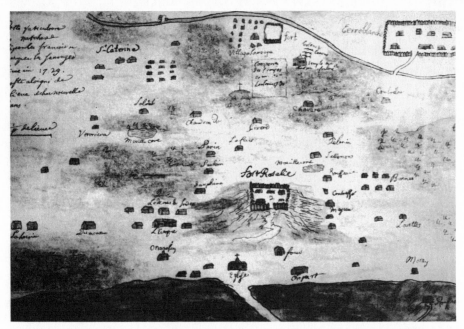

A drawing of Fort Rosalie and surrounding buildings in the late 1700s

were imported into the province, and a legal code regulating the institution of slavery was proclaimed in 1724. That code, known as the Code Noire, or Black Code, was drafted by Bienville. It prohibited the separation of slave wives and husbands and banned the separation of children under age 14 from their mothers. Slaves who were freed by their owners became naturalized French citizens with all the rights and privileges of Frenchmen. The Black Code also prohibited Jews from migrating to the colony and established Roman Catholicism as the official state church of Louisiana.

One primary objective of John Law's company was the promotion of agriculture in the Natchez District, an objective achieved with a measure of success. Natchez farmers produced rice, wheat, indigo, cotton and tobacco, and by 1727 had approximately 6,000 acres in production. Tobacco, the District's most important money crop, was deemed by many to be superior to the strains that had been developed in the Virginia Tidewater region; French officials offered subsidies to encourage its production.

Because of the increase in the white population and

Left, tobacco, a crop grown on more than 260 farms during Natchez's Spanish era, and, right, indigo, planted for export in the early 1790s in Natchez

the encroachment of agriculture on their tribal lands, resentment of the French among the Natchez naturally deepened. After the British began trading with the Natchez, tribal leaders were eventually divided into pro-French and pro-English factions. The Great Sun and his brother, the war chief, were pro-French. However, by 1728 both of them had died, and the pro-English faction was very influential in promoting the 1729 rebellion.

Tribal leaders in both factions also saw the relentless erosion of their sacred traditions and witnessed the corruption and exploitation of their young men and women. In a final desperate act to save their way of life, they laid the plans for that fateful strike against Fort Rosalie, while the French schemed and dreamed of profit.

It is ironic that in 1731, the same year that the Natchez were being destroyed, the Company of the Indies collapsed. The exaggerated promises of high returns failed to materialize, and thousands of Frenchmen who speculated in its stock went into bankruptcy. John Law was driven from office and fled the country for his own safety.

After the destruction of the Natchez tribe and the failure of John Law's scheme, the Natchez District became virtually uninhabited. Fort Rosalie, which been rebuilt in 1730, was no longer occupied, and the Natchez District was summarily abolished when the French crown resumed proprietorship over the Louisiana Province. For the next 30 years Natchez remained a distant outpost in the dwindling French empire. By 1751 a traveller found only a few "lonely soldiers" living below the bluffs at Natchez.

After England defeated France in the Seven Years' War (1756-1763), France ceded to Great Britain all of its American empire that was east of the Mississippi River, except New Orleans. The French territory west of the Mississippi River, plus New Orleans, was awarded to her ally, Spain. Great Britain also obtained Florida from Spain. Consequently, in 1763, the Natchez region became a part of the British empire.

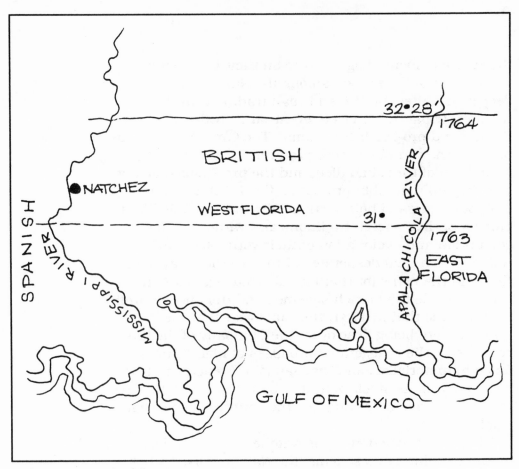

British West Florida

By a royal proclamation issued in 1763, England created a new colony called British West Florida. The northern boundary of the new colony was the 31st parallel; the southern border was the Gulf of Mexico and the east-west boundaries were the Apalachicola and the Mississippi Rivers. The eastern half of Florida comprised the colony of British East Florida. The new English territory north of the 31st parallel was closed to white settlement until England could make treaties with the Indians occupying that vast frontier. However, British officials had mistakenly included the Natchez settlement in the "off limits" area. Consequently, the Proclamation of 1763 was amended in 1764, and the northern boundary of British West Florida was moved up to the 32° 28' parallel.

Fort Panmure (first called Fort Rosalie) depicted by the artist Collot about 1796

Fort Rosalie was renamed Fort Panmure by the British, who maintained a small military garrison there. Natchez prospered under British rule, and the population steadily increased. During the years 1766-1769, a total of 39 land grants were made in the Natchez region. Most of those grants went to former British officers in payment for their services during the Seven Years' War. The grants varied in size from 20,000 acres (which went to the Earl of Eglinton) to 140 acres. Daniel Clark Sr. and John Blommart, both later prominent players in the early history of Natchez, received 3,000 acres and 1,000 acres, respectively.

A new series of land grants, much more liberal than earlier ones, was awarded in 1773. Col. Anthony Hutchins, a former British military officer, and his associates received 152,000 acres. Another 150,000 acres went to a group of Connecticut veterans of the Seven

Years' War, including Phineas and Thaddeus Lyman, Isreal and Rufus Putnam and Roger Enos. Thousands of additional acres were granted to proprietors who promised to bring settlers to the new British colony, but few of those visionary schemes ever materialized.

One of the ventures that did succeed was led by Samuel Swayzey, a Congregational minister from New Jersey who received a grant of 20,000 acres. Swayzey's group established the "Jersey Settlement" on the Homochitto River southeast of Natchez. The increasing number of British immigrants from the older colonies on the Atlantic coast eventually resulted in the dominance of the Anglican Church and the decline of Catholicism in Natchez.

In February 1776, Gov. Peter Chester of British West Florida ordered that a town be laid out at the Natchez landing. At the time there was a much greater distance between the Natchez bluff and the river's edge than there is in the late 20th century, because the great river has

Natchez Under-the-Hill depicted by the artist Montule, about 1800

widened its banks considerably over the years. Within a year after the town was laid out, there were 10 log houses and two frame houses below the bluff, with four mercantile houses in operation at the landing. Among the first merchants at the original town of Natchez were John Blommart and James Willing, whom one historian called a "well-educated but dissipated young man from an influential Philadelphia family." Both merchants also owned about 1,000 acres above the bluff. Another merchant, Louis Le Fleur, operated a prosperous boat shuttle between Natchez and Pensacola. Le Fleur later became famous both as the father of the Choctaw chieftain Greenwood Leflore and as the founder of Le Fleur's Bluff on the Pearl River, which eventually became Jackson and the state capital.

Hutchins, a veteran of the Seven Years' War and Natchez's largest land owner, was appointed the new town's Justice of the Peace, which under British law was a very powerful position. Still another important early settler was John Ellis, who soon established a large estate at nearby White Cliffs. Ellis was a member of the Royal Society of London and owned one of the largest and most impressive collections of books in the Natchez region. He, Hutchins and William Dunbar, whose handsome estate was just south of Natchez, were original members of that small but widening circle of Natchez aristocrats who eventually achieved a level of sophistication, grace and gentility that became the stuff of legends.

The population of the new town of Natchez and the surrounding area was growing so rapidly that in 1776 the English colonial office created the Natchez District as a subdivision of British West Florida. The Natchez District comprised the territory below the confluence of the Yazoo and Mississippi rivers down to a 40-mile stretch along the Gulf Coast. This triangular-shaped district, which was similar in size and shape to the Natchez District created by the French, was among the most prosperous areas of British West Florida.

Since most of the Natchez land grants went to former

English officers and soldiers, the residents of Natchez did not initially embrace the American Revolution of the 13 American colonies. Consequently, many loyalists in the older colonies fled to West Florida, where they were cordially welcomed by Gov. Chester.

The Mississippi River was an important if not indispensable trade route between the American colonies on the Atlantic and Spanish New Orleans, where the fledgling American democracy was being sold arms and other supplies by Spanish officials who saw the American Revolution as an opportunity to recapture their Florida territory from Great Britain. Because of Natchez's strategic location on the river, the Continental Congress sent an expeditionary force to the town to enlist the support of Natchez residents or at least to induce their neutrality. Led by James Willing, the "well-educated but dissipated young man" and former merchant of Natchez, the expedition soon took on the character of a raid. Willing's ragtag army of riffraff sailed from Pittsburgh to Natchez in the spring of 1778 by way of the Ohio River. They were aboard the gunboat Rattletrap, whose name was most appropriate to the participants.

When Willing arrived in Natchez he required its residents to take an oath pledging not to aid or abet the enemies of the United States. Several prominent Natchez citizens, including Hutchins, refused to take the oath. After confiscating Hutchins' property, Willing then plundered his way to New Orleans, taking Hutchins with him as a prisoner of war. On the way to New Orleans he looted several plantations, including the estate of William Dunbar, who wrote of Willing's raiders: "All was fish that came in their path." While selling his bounty in New Orleans, Willing learned that Natchez residents had broken their pledge of neutrality. He sent a detachment under Richard Harrison to Natchez, but a group of citizens led by Hutchins, who in the meantime had escaped, met and defeated Harrison near White Cliffs on April 6, 1778.

The cooperation which Spanish authorities in New Orleans afforded Willing strained the already tenuous peace between Spain and England, and war between the two countries was inevitable. When news of Spain's declaration of war against Great Britain finally arrived in New Orleans in July 1779, the governor of Spanish Louisiana, Barnardo de Galvez, moved quickly and successfully, first against Baton Rouge, then Natchez and then Florida. The 80 English grenadiers at Fort Panmure surrendered to the troops of Gov. Galvez on October 5, 1779, and Natchez came under the control of the so-called "merciful" Spanish dons. (By the 1770s Spaniards were no longer known as conquistadors but as dons, a Spanish title of respect and esteem.)

However merciful they might have claimed to be and however generous their terms of occupation, the Spanish dons were considered interlopers, unwelcome and resented, by the British subjects at Natchez. In April 1781, John Blommart, Anthony Hutchins and 200 other rebels recaptured Fort Panmure and re-established British authority in Natchez. But the rebellion was soon abandoned by its leaders when they learned that Galvez's troops had captured Mobile and Pensacola. Hutchins and several other leaders fled through the woods to Georgia and South Carolina. On June 23, 1781, the dons re-occupied Fort Panmure without opposition, took several rebel leaders prisoner and established Spanish hegemony over Natchez and its environs. The dons remained in Natchez until 1798, but their claim to the outpost was continually disputed by the young American republic.

Under the Treaty of Paris of 1783, which ended the American Revolution, the boundaries of the United States were fixed at the Mississippi River on the west and the Atlantic Coast on the east, from British Canada on the north to Spanish Florida on the south. But the exact boundary between the United States and Spanish Florida was not settled by the treaty. America claimed that the

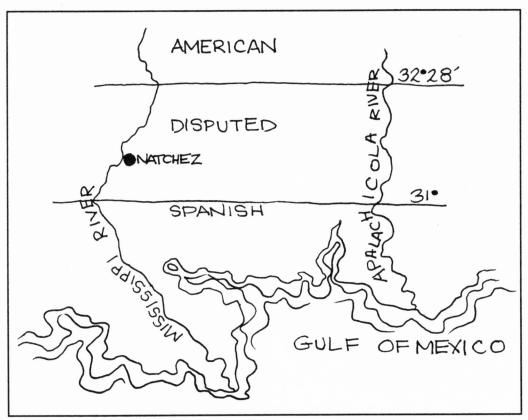

Disputed boundary lines in the 1700s

boundary between the United States and Spanish Florida
was the 31st parallel, the original northern boundary of
British West Florida, established in 1763. But Spain
claimed that the boundary was the 32° 28' parallel because the British had moved the northern boundary of
West Florida up to that line in 1764. The focus of the
dispute was Natchez. Since Spain occupied the disputed
territory and the United States was unable to validate its
claim militarily, the area between the 31st parallel and
the 32° 28' parallel remained in Spanish possession for
the next 12 years.

In spite of the conflicting claims, Natchez continued to
prosper under Spanish control. Low taxes and liberal
land grants attracted many settlers to the region, as did
religious freedom for both Jews and Protestants. Indeed,
by 1787 a majority of the district's population was English Protestant rather than Spanish Catholic. In 1789

Left, Governor of the Spanish Natchez District Manuel Gayoso de Lemos, about 1800, and, above, the mansion Concord, home of the Stephen Minor family in the early 19th century, in a photograph made about 1890

Manuel Gayoso de Lemos was appointed governor of the Natchez District. Gayoso, who had an English education and an American wife, was a popular and enlightened governor who ruled the District wisely and enjoyed the esteem of its residents. Concord, Gayoso's magnificent mansion at Natchez, was often the scene of gala balls, celebrations and other social festivities for which Natchez then and later became famous.

Fort Rosalie, dilapidated when Gayoso moved to Natchez, was not repaired. Gayoso decided to build several new forts, instead: in 1791, Fort Nogales near the present city of Vicksburg, and four years later, a fort at Chickasaw Bluffs near Memphis. Those two new forts gave Spain effective control over the Lower Mississippi River and its tributaries.

Under the dons, the Natchez District developed a diversified economy which included various manufacturing enterprises, agriculture and forestry. Livestock in the early 1790s was also an important part of the District's economy, with cattlemen raising more than 14,500 head of cattle, 5,500 sheep and 20,000 hogs. Inevitably, interests from various businessmen clashed. Certain side effects of manufacturing, for example, brought complaints from the District's cattlemen. In 1793, they complained to Gayoso that chemical waste from an indigo factory was polluting a nearby stream and was harmful to their cattle. In response to their claims, Gayoso fined the factory owners and ordered them to discontinue dumping factory residue into the local streams—one of the earliest attempts at pollution control in the New World.

As the cotton culture began to be increasingly important in the Natchez economy, Spanish authorities encouraged planters to bring their slaves into the Natchez District by offering additional and lucrative land grants to slave owners. By the mid-1790s the Natchez District's total population of approximately 4,500 people included 2,400 slaves. Male slaves were valued at about $400 each and females at about $300.

In 1795 rumors of a possible slave revolt circulated throughout the Natchez District and neighboring settlements in Louisiana. The local militia was mobilized, and Spanish authorities arrested a group of slaves at Pointe Coupee, Louisiana. After several slaves who were thought to be the leaders of the conspiracy were executed, rumors of revolt were quieted and fear bred by those rumors subsided. But these same rumors resurfaced time and again throughout the period of slavery. Southern whites lived in fear of a massive slave uprising until the institution was finally abolished.

While colonial officials were putting down a slave conspiracy in faraway Louisiana, the Spanish nation was entering the early stages of a war that, under Napoleon Bonaparte, soon enveloped all of Europe. With Spain thus distracted, America pressed its claim to Natchez

Prince Ibrahima, Natchez Slave

For 40 years, Abd al-Rahman Ibrahima, 1762-1829, was known as "Prince" among the other slaves on Thomas Foster's plantation near Natchez in Adams County, Mississippi. The nickname, "Prince," was the result of a persistent story that indeed the slave was the son of Sori, king of the Fulbe empire in Africa.

That story proved to be startlingly correct when, after Ibrahima had been a slave for nearly 20 years, he was recognized by an Irish doctor, John Cox, whose life Ibrahima and his father had saved in Africa. Ibrahima's dramatic role reversal came about when, as a colonel in his father's army in 1788, he was captured by African enemies and sold to a slave-ship captain. In Natchez he was purchased by Foster and put to work on the plantation, only to be discovered by Cox quite by accident. Eventually Ibrahima was freed and returned to West Africa.

and the disputed territory. Spain felt she was sure to lose Natchez, maybe New Orleans and perhaps even more in a war with the United States. To save as much of her American empire as possible, Spain agreed under the Treaty of San Lorenzo to relinquish her claim to all territory east of the Mississippi River and north of the 31st parallel. But to relinquish claim is not the same as giving up territory. There were several years of delay and intrigue before the flag of the young republic flew above the bluffs of Natchez.

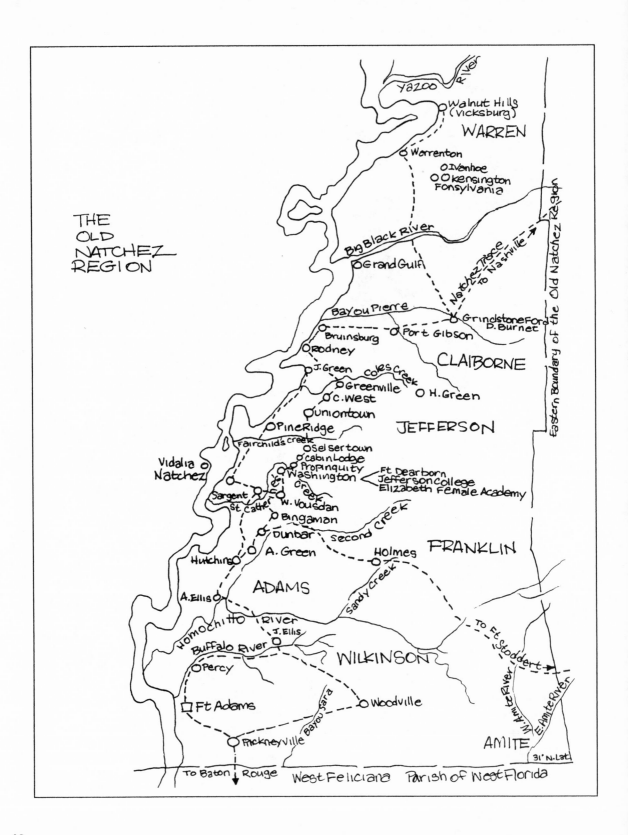

THE
OLD
NATCHEZ
REGION

YAZOO River

Walnut Hills
(Vicksburg)
WARREN

Warrenton
Ivanhoe
Kensington
Fonsylvania

Big Black River

Grand Gulf

Natchez Trace to Nashville

Eastern Boundary of the Old Natchez Region

Bayou Pierre

Grindstone Ford
D. Burnet

Bruinsburg
Rodney
Port Gibson

CLAIBORNE

J. Green
Coles Creek
Greenville
C. West
H. Green

Uniontown
JEFFERSON

Pine Ridge

Fairchild's Creek
Selsertown
Cabin Lodge
Propinquity
Washington Creek
Ft Dearborn
Jefferson College
Elizabeth Female Academy

Vidalia
Natchez

Sargent
St Cather
W. Vousdan

Bingaman

Second Creek

Dunbar

Hutchins
A. Green

Holmes
FRANKLIN

Sandy Creek

To Ft Stoddert

ADAMS

A. Ellis

Homochitto River

J. Ellis

Buffalo River

WILKINSON

Percy

W. Amite River
E. Amite River

Ft Adams

Woodville

Bayou Sara

AMITE

31° N. Lat.

Pinckneyville

To Baton Rouge   West Feliciana Parish of West Florida

42

Chapter 3

From Colonial Outpost to Territorial Capital

In the late 18th century, Natchez became a town of intrigue and a favorite rendezvous for many unsavory characters—including Spanish conspirators and American secessionists. While the American government was preoccupied with England and freedom of the seas, the great American frontier became a hatching ground for conspiracy and intrigue. Disaffected Americans in the transmontane region of Kentucky and Tennessee believed that the national government had neglected their interests and their security in favor of the Atlantic states. That disaffection was translated into threats of secession. Spain let it be known that she would subsidize the restive American frontiersmen in Kentucky and Tennessee, offering $100,000 to anyone who would instigate secession of the transmontane. There were also rumors that England from its Canadian outposts was about to mount an invasion of Spanish possessions in the Missouri Valley. Speculation even said that France, which coveted Louisiana, might reassert its claim to the American interior which La Salle had staked out a century earlier.

To protect Spain's possessions in the Lower Mississippi Valley and to provide a buffer to British encroachment on Spanish territory in the Missouri Valley, Baron de Carondolet, Spanish governor of Louisiana, wanted to establish another Spanish province extending from Natchez up to the Ohio River. To accomplish that goal, Carondolet knew it was necessary to persuade Americans in Kentucky and Tennessee to secede from the United States. If Spain failed to acquire the transmontane region, she would then favor a small independent trans-Allegheny republic which would weaken the United

States and might enable Spain to keep the Natchez District. Thus to buy the allegiance, of Kentucky tobacco farmers, or at least to encourage their disaffection, Spain gave them special trade concessions.

The economic consequences of Spanish diplomacy, however, adversely affected the Natchez economy and stirred resentment against Spain in Natchez. The trade concessions Spain gave to Kentucky tobacco farmers drove the price of Natchez tobacco to a record low and caused a severe depression in the District, a depression

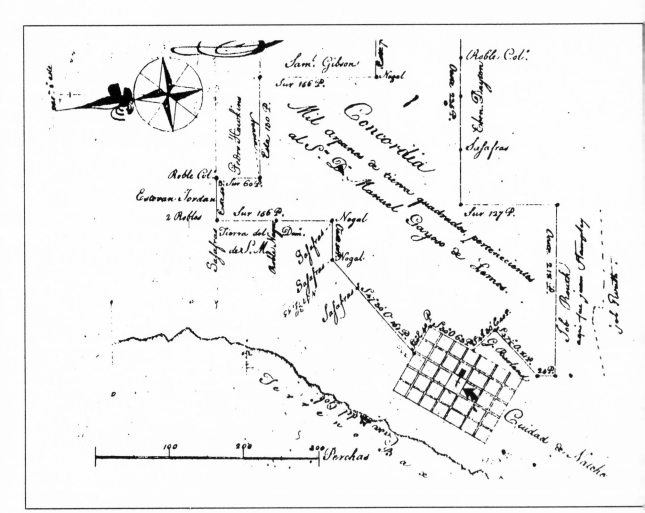

Map of the city of Natchez by William Dunbar, about 1794

which had both immediate and long-term consequences. Natchez planters became debtors, complaining bitterly to Spanish colonial authorities of high interest rates, while Natchez merchants complained of outstanding debts and defaulted accounts.

Ceaseless rumors of secession, rebellion and armed invasion during the 1790s kept the citizens of Natchez in constant turmoil. But still another element of confusion was added in 1795 when the state of Georgia asserted its claim to the territory north of the 31st parallel and began selling large parcels of that land to speculators. Georgia land claims, which superseded or at least were in conflict with earlier Spanish and English land grants, included Natchez and most of the old Natchez District.

In 1795, Natchez was an international town with citizens of Spanish, English, French and American loyalties, as well as with some citizens loyal to none save their own interests. The Natchez population was, however, predominantly American, rather than Spanish, and Protestant, rather than Catholic. Gov. Gayoso characterized the non-Spanish population as "turbulent and intriguing spirits." His assessment was seconded by Gen. James Wilkinson who, on a visit in 1798, described Natchez as an "opulent and polished community" but a town greatly "agitated by a variety of political interests and opinions."

JEFFERSON HOTEL.

THE JEFFERSON HOTEL, will be conducted in future by the Subscriber.— To the comfort and convenience of those who may board at the *Hotel*, as well as transient visitors, every attention will be paid. He will be ready, to receive his friends on Monday next, 10th inst.   JOHN BAILEY.
Natchez, Dec. 7th, 1827.   /   20

MISSISSIPPI HOTEL.

THE undersigned begs leave to inform his friends and the public in general that he has made arrangements for keeping the MISSISSIPPI HOTEL, (formerly occupied by the late Mr. John D. Gray.) He pledges himself that no exertion on his part shall be wanting to give satisfaction, and he shall make it his particular care to have his

Natchez's Jefferson Hotel and Mississippi Hotel as advertised in a Natchez newspaper about 1827

Wilkinson was surely one of the world's first double agents. He accepted payment from Spain to promote secession among the American frontiersmen. Then, while receiving payments from Spain, he accepted an appointment in the military service of the young republic and apparently conducted counterespionage against his former benefactors. Philip Nolan, a coadjutor with Wilkinson, was a Texas wrangler, horse trader and adventurer. He was also the son-in-law of Bernard Lintot, a prominent Natchez planter and merchant. (Nolan's name later became inadvertently linked to Edward Everette Hale's famous 19th-century story, "The Man Without a Country.") Both Wilkinson and Nolan were frequent visitors to Natchez in the late 1790s, but their particular roles in the various entangling conspiracies still remain a mystery.

Although overshadowed by grander schemes of more ambitious rogues, Natchez also had everyday problems of cattle rustling, highway robbery and piracy. Street brawling in Natchez became so prevalent that Gayoso issued a ban on knives and other metal weapons, but an illicit trade kept the ruffians well supplied.

Because of the special character of Natchez, a tiny town deep in the Southern forest, street brawling sometimes took on both international and theological implications. Soon after Gayoso relaxed a prohibition against public preaching by Protestant clergy, a Baptist minister, John Hannah, castigated Spain in general and the Holy Catholic Church in particular. When news of his castigation reached the streets, he was "roughed-up" by a group of Irish Catholics from Under-the-Hill. As he was being dragged past a group of Americans, he shouted, "Help me, citizens of the United States."

In spite of all that the imperial powers could do to acquire the transmontane region, it remained American, and eventually the Spanish were forced to evacuate Natchez. Andrew Ellicott was an American agent sent by President George Washington to negotiate the Spanish withdrawal and to survey the 31st parallel. He arrived at Natchez on February 24, 1797, accompanied by a small detachment of American soldiers and a cadre of woodsmen who were to assist him in marking the boundary between the United States and Spanish Florida. When the Spaniards declined to move out of Natchez immediately, the commander of the military detachment, Lieutenant Percy "Crazy" Pope, urged Ellicott to allow him to drive the stubborn dons from Natchez. But a more peaceful solution was found, and the Spanish withdrew on March 30, 1798. One week later the U. S. Congress established the Mississippi Territory.

The statute establishing the nation's newest territory was patterned after the Northwest Ordinance of 1787, with one notable exception: the Northwest Ordinance prohibited slavery north of the Ohio River. The law creating the Mississippi Territory legalized slavery as chattel property, which meant that slaves were by law personal property in the same way that household possessions or livestock were chattel goods or property. With Kentucky's admission as a slave state in 1792 and Tennessee's in 1796, and then with the legalization of slavery in Mississippi, a precedent was set at that early date. Slavery would not exist above the Ohio River, but it would below.

Andrew Ellicott locating the United States boundary line at Natchez

Natchez, the oldest continuous settlement on the lower Mississippi River and the first port of entry into the American Southwest, in 1798 became the first capital of the Mississippi Territory and the first and only county seat of Adams County. In 1802, due largely to political factionalism, the capital was moved to Washington, a town then six miles east of Natchez's outskirts.

Natchez in 1798 was literally and figuratively a town of two stories. For many years the landing below the bluffs was a community of cutthroats and prostitutes, of boatmen and brigands, of transients and fugitives, where commerce of all kinds flourished. Already renowned as Natchez Under-the-Hill, it was the origin of the Natchez Trace, an ancient, 450-mile overland artery known by many as "the Devil's Backbone," which linked Natchez

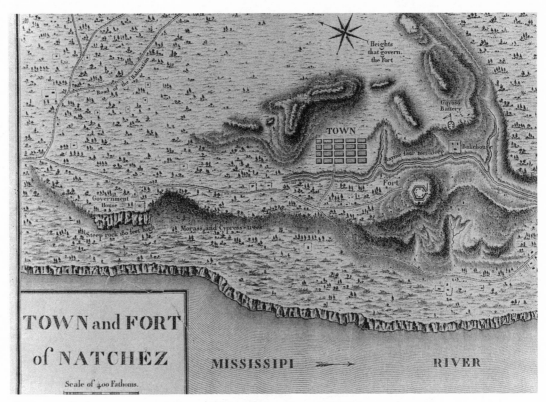

A map of the town and fort of Natchez about 1794

and Nashville, Tennessee. The upper town, Natchez on the bluff, platted in 1791, was widely known for its fine mansions and patrician elegance. It soon eclipsed the fame of Natchez's lower half, though both found an easy journey into lore and legend.

In 1803 the territorial legislature incorporated the town of Natchez, which then had a population of approximately 1,400. City government consisted primarily of a mayor, town clerk and three aldermen. These officers also constituted the mayor's court, which could try both civil and criminal cases, administer fines up to $50 and authorize up to 39 lashes, six hours in the public stocks and three hours in the pillory. All tax-paying white male citizens or members of the militia who were at least 21 years old were eligible to vote in city elections.

Municipal records of early Natchez indicate that a paid

city employee was designated as the "overseer of the poor." His primary duty was to administer the city's special funds for "orphans, destitute widows and minors." Those records also show that one-third of the city's expenditures from 1803 to 1817 were allocated to the "relief of the poor sick." Health care in general was a high priority among Natchez residents; in 1805 city fathers built the Natchez Hospital. The three-story brick building, with a 70-patient capacity, served the indigent, the general population and, normally, the local slave population. After Mississippi was admitted to statehood in 1817, the hospital began receiving state funds, and in 1836 its name was changed to State Hospital of Mississippi.

The two great calamities that most often plagued antebellum towns were fires and epidemics. Largely because Natchez established strict building codes to minimize the possibility of fires, the town escaped the first great danger and experienced only slight problems with epidemics. Very early the town established a "city watch," which consisted of a committee to look for early signs of communicable diseases. The committee was empowered to quarantine individuals who were suspected of having such diseases. The town also built a small quarantine hospital two miles to the south where persons with contagious diseases could be isolated from the general population.

Natchez, a mecca for lawyers, was the city where some of the state's most distinguished attorneys and jurists got their start. Early court records of Natchez also bear out the adage that "America is a litigious society." In April 1803, eight lawyers were admitted to the Natchez bar. Within the next two years, 144 lawsuits were filed. That means that one out of every 10 people in Natchez was sued or that some people were sued several times.

One of the most intriguing episodes of early Natchez history is the Burr conspiracy; historians have yet to resolve the mystery that cloaked Burr's mission. In the

Aaron Burr, vice president of the United States, 1801-1805, who was arrested and then freed when he visited Natchez in 1807

fall of 1806, rumors circulated throughout the Old Southwest that Aaron Burr, former vice-president and the famous duelist who killed Alexander Hamilton, was leading an expeditionary force down the Mississippi River. President Thomas Jefferson issued a proclamation warning the citizens of the Southwest to beware of "the treasonable expedition." Precisely what Burr's intentions were, neither the rumors nor the presidential proclamation made clear. Consequently, an alarmed and somewhat agitated populace gave way to wild speculation.

Some believed that Burr and the infamous Gen. James Wilkinson, who had previously been implicated in a secessionist plot in Kentucky, were planning a rebellion in America's newly acquired Louisiana Territory. Others speculated that Great Britain, which still hoped to regain her lost American colonies, was instigating the treachery and subsidizing the conspirators. Some rumors had Burr and Wilkinson invading Spanish territory beyond the Sabine River, possibly even Mexico itself.

Mississippi's Acting Gov. Cowles Mead, fearing an imminent invasion of the Mississippi Territory, called out the militia and arrested Dr. John F. Carmichael, a prominent Natchez citizen who was believed to be in cahoots with Burr. On January 10, 1807, Burr's flotilla of nine unarmed ships and 75 men docked just upriver from Natchez. Maj. Ferdinand Claiborne, head of the militia, soon took Burr and the other "restless spirits" into custody. Judge Thomas Rodney empaneled a grand jury to present formal charges against Burr and set a hearing for February 2. Bond, set at $10,000, was raised by some of Burr's many friends at Natchez. Lyman Harding, a Natchez attorney, agreed to represent Burr at the hearing. Burr was a man of rare social grace and great charm, and during his brief stay in Natchez he became the toast of the town.

American statesman Alexander Hamilton, about 1803

On February 2, 1807, a "large and curious crowd" gathered in the territorial capital on the day Burr was to appear before the grand jury. The hearing was presided over by Judge Thomas Rodney and Judge Peter Bryan Bruin, an inebriate who was later removed from the bench. George Poindexter, Territorial Attorney General, startled the curious crowd by asking the judges to dismiss the defendant on the grounds that the territorial court had no jurisdiction in the matter. His motion was denied, and vague charges of conspiracy to commit treason were made against Burr. The grand jury quickly found in favor of Burr, its foreman scolding territorial officials for arresting Burr without a proper warrant. Burr interrupted the court momentarily, speaking out loudly that he "quite agreed" with the jury. Burr partisans in the court room roared with laughter.

Mississippi Territorial leader George Poindexter of Natchez, about 1817

For some still unknown reason Burr absconded from Natchez shortly after his hearing; later he was arrested near Mobile. He disguised himself in buckskins, but his aristocratic bearing and speech—and the handsome steed provided by a Natchez friend—betrayed him. He was taken into custody by federal authorities and escorted to Richmond, Virginia, where he was tried in the U.S. Supreme Court on the charge of treason. Chief Justice John Marshall dropped the charges and released Burr when his chief accuser, President Thomas Jefferson, refused to appear before the court. Following his trial, Burr spent a brief sojourn in Europe and then returned to the United States to practice law in New York until his death in 1836.

It seems almost inevitable that an episode of such intrigue and mystery would include a tragic love story. And indeed it did. While in Natchez, Burr was given lodging by an old friend from the American Revolution, Col. Benijah Osman, at his plantation near Half-way Hill. There the love story took place. A century later that tale of romance and sorrow was told in the florid language of Mississippi's Methodist Bishop, Charles Betts Galloway:

> Situated on the summit of the hill was a modest, vine-covered cottage, where dwelt a widow from Virginia and her rarely beautiful daughter, Madeline. She was an only child and a 'miracle of beauty.' Into the innocent ear of that lovely maiden Aaron Burr, with bewitching eloquence, poured the story of his love. She was charmed and enchained by the sorcery of his smooth, persuasive speech, and the heart that had never been touched before could not resist his magic power. Against all the promptings of reason and her better nature she yielded her hand to his and gave him the covenant and pledge of an innocent heart. That night, after leaving Colonel Osman's, he stopped at the cottage and implored the beautiful maiden to accompany him in his flight. He promised marriage, fortune and fame, but the pure and proud-spirited girl successfully resisted. She could not compromise the purity of her stainless character. The accomplished deceiver never returned and sorrow never entirely went out of poor Madeline's heart.

Windy Hill Manor, Col. Benijah Osman's plantation house on Half-way Hill, in a 1940 photograph

As all great love stories should, Madeline's had a happy ending. Historian J. F. H. Claiborne writes that she "was wooed by many a lover" and that "fortunes and the homage of devoted hearts were laid at her feet." But "the maid of Half-way Hill remained true to her absent lover," sustained by "the recollections of his manly beauty." After Burr had fallen into misfortune he at last released Madeline from her pledge and urged her to "enter a convent." Several years later, as a companion to "a lady of large fortune," Madeline traveled to Havana where her "beauty, grace and elegance produced the greatest enthusiasm." She was "feted by the governor-general and the daily homage to her beauty never ceased until the evening bells sounded the Angelus." Claiborne tells us that "without surrendering her heart, she returned to the cottage on the Half-way Hill." But she was followed there "by Mr. K, an English gentleman, the head of the largest commercial house in Havana, and to him, on the second visit, she gave her hand."

The town that embraced Burr so warmly and feted him so graciously was unique in the American frontier experience. Although it was located on America's far western frontier, Natchez was not a frontier town struggling to civilize itself. In its early years Natchez was the intellectual and cultural center of the American Southwest, and among its diverse population were men and women of wealth, elegance and learning who created a society of refinement that existed perhaps nowhere else on America's vast frontier.

The Natchez Theatre Association presented locally produced theatrical performances on a regular basis as well as touring professional groups. One of America's earliest state-supported colleges, Jefferson College, was established at nearby Washington in 1802, and several other schools of various levels were conducted in Natchez and Washington.

In 1803 a literary and scientific club, the Mississippi Society for the Acquirement and Dissemination of Useful Knowledge, was established. William Dunbar, a charter

Drawing of the Natchez Theatre by Tyrone Power, about 1850

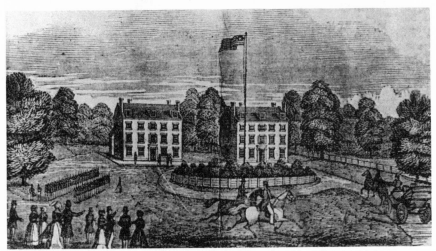

Jefferson College, chartered in 1802

*William Dunbar,
an influential,
well-educated
Natchez leader,
about 1800*

member, imported a large and powerful telescope.
Dunbar generously shared the wonders of his marvelous
instrument with local townspeople, among whom it was
extremely popular, especially on those rare occasions
when "shooting stars" and comets could be seen darting
across Southern skies.

But one local evangelical minister was not so impressed. He scolded Dunbar for "prying on the privacy of
the Almighty." Dunbar, a scientist of some renown, was
a member of the American Philosophical Society and a
correspondent with Thomas Jefferson. He also conducted several scientific expeditions into the Louisiana
Territory, which America had acquired by purchase in
1803.

Andrew Marschalk of Natchez, editor of the *Mississippi
Herald* and called the "father of Mississippi journalism,"
kept a reading room where the learned gentlemen of

Natchez and Washington could browse through the latest gazettes, new books and maps and engage in friendly as well as unfriendly disputation. He was joined by other learned citizens of early Natchez and Washington, including David Ker, school master and former president of the University of North Carolina; Dr. Rush Nutt, who in 1833 developed the leading Petit Gulf cotton seed; Solomon Turnipseed, a Fellow of the Royal Society; John and Lucy Audubon; and the Rev. Lorenzo Dow, Mississippi's most fascinating circuit rider.

Andrew Marschalk, Mississippi's first printer, about 1820

Many of the learned men of Natchez were also sporting men, and the "sport of kings" was among their favorite diversions. Several tracks and jockey clubs existed in Natchez and neighboring Wilkinson County. Natchez's Fleetwood and Pharsalia were two of the favorite tracks where aristocrats raced their thoroughbreds and sometimes made side bets of up to $10,000 or 500 bales of cotton or perhaps even more. Horse racing, also a popular pastime of Natchez Under-the-Hill, was conducted there in a less formal and gracious atmosphere, but the stakes in comparison to those in the city of Natchez were just as high and the excitement just as thrilling.

Early Methodist circuit preacher Lorenzo Dow, about 1820

Like horse racing, politics was a favorite pastime in territorial Natchez. Factional lines drawn in those early years delineated Mississippi politics until the Civil War. Factional politics in early Natchez, and indeed throughout Mississippi during the antebellum years, were bitter and acrimonious. Newspapers were party organs, and editorial diatribes against the opposition

SPORTSMEN
TAKE NOTICE.

THE Fleet Field RACES commence on Thursday the 1st of January next, as notified by hand bills sometime past circulated.

The subscribers will be pleased to meet on Saturday the 20th inst. on the turf, for the purpose of nominating different persons to superintend the RACES, and make such other regulations as are materially necessary for carrying the same into effect.

A horse race notice in a Natchez newspaper of 1800

A widely read Natchez newspaper, The Ariel, *in 1826*

often prompted fist fights and duels. The two contending
factions were the Federalists, whose political and economic principles were formulated by Alexander
Hamilton, and the Democratic-Republicans, who embraced the political ideology of Thomas Jefferson. The
Federalists later became the Whigs, under the leadership
of Henry Clay and Daniel Webster. The Democratic-
Republicans eventually became the Jacksonian Democrats, whose hero was Andrew Jackson. The Whigs
represented the interests of the wealthy planter and
merchant class, while the Jacksonian Democrats represented the "common man."

Although the seat of government during the territorial
period did not remain in Natchez (it moved to Washington in 1802), and although the seat of government after
statehood likewise did not remain in Natchez, (it moved
to Jackson in 1822), Natchez continued to be the cultural and economic capital of Mississippi. The city's
influence and affluence were derived both from the

NATCHEZ

First settled by French,
1716-29. Lasting growth
came with Britain, 1763-
1779, and Spain, 1779-98.
Cotton and trade made it
commercial and cultural
capital of Old South.

*Highway marker
noting Natchez's
history, erected by
the Mississippi De-
partment of Archives
and History*

cotton culture and the fact that the town was the center of the emerging cotton kingdom. James Wilkins, a Natchez banker and broker who also owned approximately 5,000 acres of land and nearly 300 slaves, was the state's largest cotton commissioner. According to historian J. F. H. Claiborne, Wilkins "controlled the commerce of Mississippi, and nearly all the cotton it produced." In 1815 Natchez and Adams County provided 32 percent of Mississippi's revenue, with the seven counties of the Old Natchez District providing 74 percent.

After the collapse of the tobacco industry in the 1790s, Natchez planters turned to indigo, but it failed to develop into a lucrative money crop. Cotton seemed to be the most promising cash crop, but it had two major problems. First, there was no efficient way of separating cotton lint from the seeds. The roller gin, which was then in use, could produce only about 75 pounds a day, not enough to make cotton a profitable money crop. The other problem was that the existing strains of cotton were not suitable to the warm, damp climate of Natchez. Consequently, for cotton to become a profitable cash crop, a new ginning process and a cotton variety compatible with a wet climate had to be developed.

The first of those problems was solved unexpectedly by a Yankee tutor who knew little of cotton and planting. In 1795 Eli Whitney designed a gin that used a rotating cylinder with wire brushes to separate lint from seed. This new gin, which could produce from 500 to 1,000 pounds of lint a day, was modified and improved by a Natchez blacksmith and slave mechanic named Barclay and was soon in use throughout the Natchez District. This machine, so simple and so easy to reproduce, realized very little income for Whitney, although it profoundly influenced the course of American history.

Within a year after Whitney's new process was developed, David Greenleaf built the first public gin at Selsertown, a small community northeast of Natchez. About that same time William Dunbar, also of Natchez, invented the screw press and was soon experimenting

Eli Whitney's cotton gin, about 1794

with an iron press that shaped the raw cotton lint into square bales. Natchez's fabled cotton kingdom was just emerging in 1798, when Dunbar wrote, "We continue to cultivate cotton with very great success. It is by far the most profitable crop we have ever undertaken." In 1800 Natchez exported 3 million pounds of the "white gold."

Soon after the invention of the cotton gin and the screw press, Dr. Rush Nutt of Natchez developed a new variety of cotton that was suitable to the Natchez climate. Known as the Petit Gulf variety, it was developed from Mexican seed which, according to a local folk tale, was smuggled out of Mexico in 1807 by Walter Burling who hid the seeds in several dolls.

As if history conspired to shape the destiny of this Natchez country, the two chief obstacles to a lucrative cotton culture were finally resolved, and the Old South entered a new age of agriculture. Cotton was crown prince. It would soon be king.

After the War of 1812 the population of the Mississippi Territory increased rapidly; the area became eligible for statehood in 1817. The Mississippi Territory in the early 1800s included the present states of Mississippi and Alabama. Because the area was so large, all parties agreed that the Territory would have to be divided, but there was bitter controversy over how that division should be made. Scattered eastern settlements near the Tombigbee River wanted the Territory divided into two equal parts by a line running east and west. By this plan the northern half would constitute one state and the southern half another. That divisional arrangement would place the Tombigbee settlements in the state with Natchez.

But the residents of Natchez, especially the wealthy planters and merchants, did not want to be linked with what they considered the quarrelsome and backward settlements of the Tombigbee region. They preferred a line running north to south, giving each state land bordering the Gulf of Mexico, and dividing the Territory into eastern and western sections. Eventually, the Natchez position prevailed, and in 1817 the Mississippi Territory was equally divided by a line running from Tennessee down to the Gulf Coast. On December 10, 1817, the western half became the state of Mississippi, and in 1819 the eastern half became Alabama.

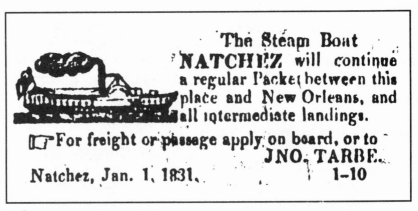

The Steam Boat NATCHEZ will continue a regular Packet between this place and New Orleans, and all intermediate landings.

For freight or passage apply on board, or to

JNO. TARBE.

Natchez, Jan. 1, 1831.   1–10

An 1831 advertisement for the steamboat Natchez

Chapter 4

King Cotton and the Grandeur of Old Natchez

Almost everyone in antebellum Natchez was connected to cotton by buying, selling, picking, planting or supplying the voracious demands of that lucrative crop. That was especially true after the flush times of the 1830s when, according to Joseph Glover Baldwin, "Prosperity covered the land with a golden canopy (and) the cotton plantation whitened the earth." In 1838 Natchez planters produced and shipped more than 40,000 bales (or, 20 million pounds) to Liverpool and Boston. During those years of prosperity, the Crown Prince became King Cotton. His retainers were legion.

White gold

Cotton may have been a profitable cash crop, but credit fueled the engine that drove the process of production. As much as 70 percent of the cotton-related business transactions in Natchez was done on credit. The almost insatiable demands of King Cotton caused Natchez bankers to scurry. During the 1830s there were four banks in Natchez, including a branch of the Bank of the United States. Those banks failed, however, during the depression caused by the Panic of 1837. After the crash, planters and plain folks alike were skeptical of banks; most of them preferred to do business with W. A. Britton and Company, an exchange brokerage that became the principal financial institution in Natchez during the 1840s. After George Koontz became associated with Britton and Company in the 1850s, banking was the company's primary business.

Cotton production was both a lucrative and a labor-intensive enterprise. The crop required constant care from its planting in the early spring until it was "laid by" in the late summer. Then again, care was required during the fall picking season. The Southern plantation system, employing slave labor, required that the region's expanding economy be dependent on a continuing supply of slaves. Before the cotton boom of the 1830s, the chief benefits of slave ownership were economic. But to the second and third generation of aristocrats, those who inherited great wealth, slavery became something more than an economic institution or a labor system. The trappings of aristocracy and the ornaments of wealth, and, above all, the social rank which the planter class enjoyed, made slave-owning a way of life for a privileged few.

One of the ironies of Southern history is that the slave system was most ardently defended by whites who owned no slaves. To the non-slave-holding class of Southern whites, slavery was a social mechanism that regulated the relationship between dominant and subservient classes and regularized behavior patterns for both races.

CREDIT SALE OF A CHOICE GANG OF 41
SLAVES!
COMPRISING MECHANICS, LABORERS, ETC,

FOR THE SETTLEMENT OF A CO-PARTNERSHIP OF RAILROAD CONTRACTORS.

BY J. A. BEARD & MAY, J. A. BEARD, AUCT'R.

WILL BE SOLD AT AUCTION, AT BANKS' ARCADE, MAGAZINE STREET,

ON TUESDAY, FEBRUARY 5th, 1856,

AT 12 O'CLOCK.

Notice of slave sale in Natchez in 1856

Recent scholarship has corrected many myths and misconceptions about the Southern slave system. The most enduring myth about slavery is that all slaves and all slave owners were alike. The truth is that "each plantation was a law unto itself" and that neither the slave nor the slave-owner was a mindless player in a system of fixed relationships. On the contrary, the dynamics of the slave-and-master relationship was shaped by the interaction between living human beings.

The owner's mastery over his slaves was not as complete as he might have believed or as some historians have concluded. The slaveholder could exact compliance and compel the slave's outward behavior, but slaves were not powerless to influence and improve their own conditions. They could slow down production, break tools, set fire to fields, abuse livestock or feign illness to show their discontent and induce the owner or overseer to relax the regimen.

Though the lash may have been the slave owner's symbol of authority, it was not the whip or the pain that subdued the slave. It was the absence of any effective legal or social restraint or limit on the owner's absolute control over their lives. Slaves knew that the white man's will or whim was final. There was no appeal of it or escaping from it, except to run away.

Not all slave owners were persuaded by the philosophical and theological arguments justifying human bondage.

Sunday afternoon on the plantation, about 1830

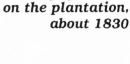

Isaac Ross of Jefferson County near Natchez, who manumitted his slaves and helped them return to Africa

One such heretic was Capt. Isaac Ross of nearby Jefferson County, whose will manumitted his slaves and provided for their return to Liberia, a small independent republic on the west coast of Africa. Liberia was established under the auspices of the American Colonization Society, which initiated the repatriation of free blacks.

Judge James Green was an Adams County planter who had also freed his slaves and provided for their return to Liberia. Green's former slaves established a settlement called "Mississippi in Africa." But Isaac Ross's slaves were not as fortunate as Judge Green's had been. Some of the Ross heirs contested the will and for 12 years prevented its execution. Finally, the Ross heirs who were sympathetic to the captain's design deeded their slaves to Stephen Duncan of Natchez, who helped them slip away to New Orleans, where they began their journey back to Africa.

A Mississippi branch of the American Colonization Society was established in Natchez in 1831 by Stephen

Duncan, David Ker, David Hunt and several other large slave holders. The Mississippi Colonization Society arranged for 571 free blacks from the Natchez area to return to Africa. But as the agitation over abolition intensified in the 1840s, the Mississippi Legislature passed a law prohibiting the manumission of slaves, and the Colonization Society disbanded.

Natchez, already in its second century when the cotton boom began, soon became one of the Cotton Kingdom's wealthiest and most sophisticated provinces. But Old Natchez was a town of two stories, or, as one newspaper put it, there was "Natchez proper, and Natchez improper." During the antebellum years Natchez Under-the-Hill was generally considered the wickedest waterfront on the Great River. One visitor wrote, "For the size of it, there is not, perhaps in the world, a more profligate place." Another said it was "hell on earth, with bells attached."

On a busy day at that infamous landing there were as many as 400 vessels ranging from ocean liners to flatboats, all of which, one historian remarked, were "moored in a bobbing, shifting line" as their crews "cursed each other and jockeyed for space." On the wharf, unsuspecting visitors were lured to gambling dens and pleasure palaces on Silver Street, where "half-nude girls bent out of windows, touting their charms." In that "paradise of individualism, a man took what he wanted or what he could grab [and] kept what he caught until some hardier bucko came along and strangled or gutted him for it."

The Natchez Temperance Society, which published a newspaper called The Cold Water Man, promoted the enactment of an 1839 state law that prohibited the sale of liquor in quantities under one gallon. But neither the Society nor the law got much respect below the bluff. Sometimes the good people of Natchez proper conducted cleanups at "Natchez improper." Vigilantes apprehended and hanged thugs and gamblers, burned their shacks and besought prostitutes to be more circumspect.

*Natchez
Under-the-Hill
before the
Civil War*

Some claim that the Great River, in revenge against the place that shamed its name, altered its course, widened its banks and gobbled up much of that awful place. They also say that the tornado of 1840, which lashed the bluffs with its angry winds, was another natural act of retribution. No matter what, eventually, Natchez Under-the-Hill was tamed, not by law or nature but by the railroad that linked New Orleans with Chicago, bypassing Natchez. The locomotive superseded the steamboat, the boxcar replaced the flatboat and Natchez Under-the-Hill slipped into legend while its crumbling loess bluffs slid into the sea.

Although the waterfront may have given Natchez a bad name, the Great River was the city's lifeline and link to the world's marketplace, where Natchez cotton sold dear. Flatboats, keelboats and even the small "Allegheny skiffs," which one observer could not assign to any "specific class of boats," remained important to the Natchez economy throughout most of the antebellum period.

In 1811 a new age of river travel dawned when Nicholas Roosevelt docked his steamboat, New Orleans, at the Natchez landing during its historic journey from Pittsburgh to New Orleans. For several years afterwards, the New Orleans made regular runs along the 300-mile river stretch from New Orleans to Natchez. Roosevelt's original design, modified by Henry Shreve, had steamboats soon making round trips from New Orleans to Louisville in a then-dizzying 45 days.

Hoping to capitalize on the new technology, a group of Natchez planters organized the Natchez Steam Packet Company in 1838 and contracted with a Brooklyn shipyard to build a large cargo vessel for trans-Atlantic trips. The new ship, which they christened the Natchez, enabled Natchez planters to trade directly with European cotton merchants, eliminating shipping costs they were paying to other packet companies. The venture was not profitable, however, and the company dissolved after a few years in operation.

Steamboating on the Mississippi was both a commercial and recreational enterprise, with pleasure cruises a favorite pastime among Natchez planters and their families. Steamboat races were also extremely popular, attracting thousands of spectators along the banks of the river. Some races became legends in their own time, especially those that ended in disaster and/or the loss of many lives. During a race in 1837, 50 people were killed when the boiler of the Blackhawk exploded near the Natchez landing. In a similar accident the Ben Sherrod sank just south of Natchez with a loss of 150 lives.

Even in the heyday of steamboating, some Natchez leaders, particularly John Anthony Quitman, saw the railroad as the wave of the future. But Quitman was

One of the first railroad engines in Mississippi on the Natchez & Hamburg Railroad, about 1836

unable to organize enough interest or financial support to establish rail connections between Natchez and other Mississippi cities, such as Vicksburg and Jackson, by then the state capital.

Although the river continued to be the primary access to Natchez during the pre-Civil War years, there were several roads that linked Natchez to the interior of the state and eventually to the eastern seaboard. By far the most important of those overland routes was the Natchez Trace, which extended from Natchez up 450 miles through a bandit-infested wilderness to Nashville, Tennessee. After it was made a United States postal road in 1801, and especially after the Indians ceded their land along its route in the early 1830s, traffic on the Trace greatly increased. The notorious outlaw gangs, the Harpes, the Masons and the Murrells, were also eventually eliminated or at least restrained, and traveling on the Trace became much less dangerous.

While the bandits along the Trace and the rowdies at the Natchez landing were enlarging their reputation for bad behavior, the residents above the Natchez bluff were elaborating their own renown for social elegance. In

Jenny Lind, the "Swedish Nightingale," about 1851, the year she performed in Natchez

Natchez's Elizabeth Taylor Greenfield, the "Black Swan," about 1850, when she toured Europe and sang for royalty

1828 the Natchez Theatrical Association employed a full-time director to manage its newly constructed brick theater, which had a seating capacity of 700 and was lighted with sperm oil lamps. The year after the new theater opened, Edwin Forrest, America's foremost Shakespearean actor, played in *Hamlet* to a packed house. In 1835 the Irish idol, Tyrone Power, attracted a large audience, and in 1851, when P. T. Barnum brought Jenny Lind to Natchez, the performance was moved from the theater to the larger, 800-seat Methodist Church. The "Swedish Nightingale" sang brilliantly for an adoring and overflowing crowd, attracting a $5,000 gate.

While the "Swedish Nightingale" was serenading America, the Black Swan of Natchez was singing to Europe. Elizabeth Taylor Greenfield, born a slave in Natchez, became America's prima donna in the 1840s and 1850s. Billed as the Black Swan, her contemporaries were astonished by the range of her voice, which was said to extend from G on the bass clef to E on the treble. In the early 1850s she toured and studied in Europe, and at a command performance, sang for the Queen of England.

While the Black Swan was taking bows and singing encores, William Johnson (1809-1851), the "Barber of Natchez," for 16 years was keeping a secret, 2,000-page journal. Johnson, crown prince of a small colony of free blacks in antebellum Natchez, was a successful entrepreneur, planter and slave owner. He took refuge in his diary from a society which shut him out because he was a gentleman of color. The publication of this diary in 1951 rescued Johnson from the clutch of obscurity and forever linked him to the literati of Old Natchez, a community of enduring significance.

Residents of Old Natchez were treated to a ceaseless parade of traveling circuses, menageries and performers of all kinds, including the ever-popular dwarf Tom Thumb, who visited the city three times. Natchez also enjoyed frequent visits of statesmen and dignitaries, for whom it opened wide its gates of welcome. Only once did Old Natchez withhold its hospitality from a famous visitor. When Santa Anna stopped briefly at Natchez on his way to meet with President Andrew Jackson, he was jeered in the city that sent Felix Huston to Texas to lead the Texas army against the tyrant of Mexico.

Among the many celebrated visitors to antebellum Natchez were Louis Phillipe, the future king of France; the Marquis de Lafayette, who was a general at 19; Andrew Jackson, the hero of New Orleans and champion of the common man; Henry Clay, the great compromiser and favorite of Natchez Whigs; and Edward Everette, the Massachusetts lawyer who defended President Andrew Johnson at his impeachment trial in 1868.

Natchez visitors who did not enjoy the hospitality of a local mansion could find a measure of comfort in one of the several hotels of Natchez, which were conveniently located two or three blocks from the landing. If a gentle-

William Johnson, Free Black

William Johnson of Natchez, 1809-1851, was crown prince of a small colony of free blacks in antebellum Natchez. A successful barber, entrepreneur, planter and slave owner, he reflected on life in Natchez for 16 years in a series of secret diaries. Filled with observations, art work and doodling, the diaries were discovered and published a century after Johnson's death. Their publication as well as his biography, *The Barber of Natchez*, catapulted Johnson into fame and led to the acquisition of his State Street home by the National Park Service for the Natchez National Historical Park.

man wanted only a shave and a bath, he could find both at public bath houses and barber shops, the best of which were operated by William Johnson, Mississippi's most prosperous and most famous free man of color. At his thriving establishment on Main Street, Johnson charged two bits (25 cents) for a haircut and one bit (12 1/2 cents) for a shave.

It was generally acknowledged that William Parker's Mississippi Hotel offered the best accommodations of any hotel in the state during the 1830s. But, unfortunately for river travelers, this hotel was destroyed by the tornado of 1840. The 120 rooms of the City Hotel, which was built in 1837, were so lavish that a Natchez newspaper compared it favorably to the Astor House of New York.

Elijah Bell's Mansion House, the city's best-known hotel, was the scene of a grand ball given in honor of

Parker's Mississippi Hotel, as seen in John James Audubon's landscape of Natchez, 1822

Henry Clay on one of his visits to Natchez. One of the specialties of the Mansion House was the fabled mint julep. According to a description written by a guest who had just enjoyed a julep, the Mansion House cocktail "smelled like a bouquet." He pronounced it a "transcendent julep [which] excelled anything of the kind made on the continent of Columbus."

In addition to the hotels in Natchez proper, there were also several less commodious establishments at the landing, which offered bed, board, bar and entertainment.

While Natchez proper and Natchez improper were acquiring their disparate reputations for gaiety and graciousness, the Natchez region was also becoming known for its scientific and intellectual activities. In spite of the fact that many of the elite families sent their children away to school or kept them home and employed tutors, the town of Natchez had a very successful, well-funded public school as well as three colleges.

The city's public school, called the Natchez Institute, was built on property donated by Alvarez Fisk, a wealthy aristocrat who also gave the school several large cash donations. During the 1850s, the Institute, coeducational with 13 grade levels, enrolled as many as 750 students. More than half of the town's revenue was allocated to the school.

Jefferson College, established at the nearby town of Washington in 1802, was one of the country's earliest public institutions of higher learning. It was plagued from the beginning by financial problems, which delayed its opening until 1811 and caused its suspension on several other occasions. This college was one of the first to offer agricultural education and was among the first to adopt an elective curriculum. At the outbreak of the Civil War, Jefferson College closed; its collegiate department did not reopen after the war, although its preparatory division did.

Also located at Washington, Elizabeth Female Academy

was founded in 1818 by the Methodist Conference. It is cited by some authorities as the first degree-granting institution for women in the South and perhaps in the country. The academy survived for 29 years, closing in 1847.

About 35 miles north of Natchez, Oakland College was established near Port Gibson in 1830 under Presbyterian sponsorship. By the late 1850s Oakland College was a flourishing institution with approximately 100 students, 19 buildings and library holdings in excess of 4,000 volumes. David Ker and David Hunt, both wealthy Natchez planters, made substantial gifts to Oakland, Ker giving at least $25,000 and Hunt as much as $150,000. But like many other antebellum institutions, Oakland did not survive the Civil War. In 1871 the state of Mississippi purchased the campus and established what became Alcorn State University, one of the earliest state supported institutions of higher learning for blacks in the United States.

The faculties of the three colleges in the Natchez area, along with the distinguished members of the Natchez bar and several planters of truly uncommon learning, created in Natchez in the first half of the 19th century an intellectual climate perhaps unmatched by any other town its size in America.

Among the Natchez literati were Sarah Ellis Dorsey and Varina Howell Davis, both of whom were Natchez belles indelibly linked to Jefferson Davis; as well as Catherine Ware Warfield and Eliza Ann Dupuy.

Sarah Dorsey, a 19th-century feminist who willed her Biloxi mansion, Beauvoir, to Jefferson Davis as a retirement home, published several novels under the pen name "Filia."

Varina Howell Davis's two-volume biography of her famous husband is an indispensable resource on Jefferson Davis's tragic life. After her husband's death Mrs. Davis supported herself and her family as a freelance writer in New York.

Varina Howell Davis of Natchez, First Lady of the Confederacy, about 1846

Jefferson Davis of Mississippi, only president of the Confederate States of America, about 1855

Sarah Ellis Dorsey of Natchez, Jefferson Davis' great friend who bequeathed him her home, Beauvoir, on the Mississippi Gulf Coast

Catherine Ware Warfield's first novel, *The Household of Bouverie*, was considered by a contemporary critic as "one of the most remarkable novels ever written by an American woman."

Eliza Ann Dupuy, who was brought to Natchez to tutor Sarah Ellis Dorsey, wrote one of the first fictional accounts of Aaron Burr's life. The novel, aptly titled *The Conspirator*, sold more than 25,000 copies.

These and other women writers often read from their works at literary gatherings and have been called "ornaments in the brilliant circle of wit and intellect" that distinguished Old Natchez.

Among the men within that circle of intellect were newspaper editors Giles M. Hillyer, Lorenzo A. Bensancon and Henry Vose, whose poetry was published in more than 30 newspapers around the country. Vose also compiled a dictionary of the Choctaw Indian language and left an unpublished 2,000-page history of Mississippi when he died at age 35.

Still another intellectual was the renowned artist John

John James Audubon, a renowned naturalist and artist who taught at Elizabeth Female Academy near Natchez in 1822

James Audubon, who taught at Elizabeth Female Academy in the early 1820s while compiling his masterpiece, *The Birds of America*.

Some of the best-known early Natchez scholars and historians were John W. Monette, author of the two-volume *History of the Discovery and Settlement of the Valley of the Mississippi*; John F. H. Claiborne, biographer of Gov. John Quitman and Gen. Sam Dale and author of *Mississippi, as a Province, Territory and State*; Nathaniel Ware, father of Catherine Ware Warfield, who wrote a widely acclaimed political treatise on Whig philosophy entitled *Notes on Political Economy as Applicable to the United States*; and Leonard Gale, a professor at Jefferson College who published two college textbooks on chemistry.

The 2,000-page journal of yet another historian, William Johnson, which was published by Edwin Davis and William Hogan in 1951 as *William Johnson's Natchez: The Antebellum Diary of a Free Negro*, was considered by the 20th-century Pulitzer Prize-winning Mississippian Hodding Carter as "the most unusual personal record ever kept in the United States."

Two of the most famous literary sons of Old Natchez were Joseph Holt Ingraham and his son, Prentiss. They were by actual count America's most prolific novelists, together publishing more than 700 novels and 400 novelettes. Joseph Holt Ingraham, who taught at Jefferson College before the Civil War, also published a commentary on life in the Natchez region entitled *The South-West, by a Yankee*. Prentiss Ingraham, who was named after Natchez leader Seargent S. Prentiss, was born in Adams County in 1843 and later served in Withers' Mississippi Regiment, CSA.

Seargent Smith Prentiss of Natchez, an attorney and one of America's most gifted orators, in an 1830 portrait

Also leading figures were Benjamin L. C. Wailes, antebellum Mississippi's best-known man of science, who in 1854 published the still useful *Report on the Agriculture and Geology of Mississippi*, and Thomas Affleck, owner of Ingleside Plantation and the Southern Nurseries, which at one time included 70,000 fruit trees. Affleck also published the widely used *Cotton Plantation Record and Account Book*.

Since soil chemistry and land management were of great interest to Natchez planters, most of them were members of the Jefferson College Agricultural Society, which sponsored agricultural fairs and published the journal, Southern Planter. A literary society, known as the Lyceum, held periodic debates on scientific, educational and political topics and also published a scholarly magazine entitled *South-Western Journal, a Magazine of Science, Literature and Miscellany*.

The inner circle of the intellectual community of Old Natchez also included several members of the Natchez bar. Joseph Baldwin, who practiced law in Mississippi during the 1830s and later became a member of the California State Supreme Court, wrote of that distinguished group: "It may well be doubted if so able and efficient bar existed at any one period of the same duration in [another] Southern state."

Natchez lawyers were not only skillful practitioners, they were also successful politicians. Natchez attorneys held the governor's chair for 15 of the first 17 years; five members of the Natchez bar served on the State Supreme Court; and two were elected to the United States Senate. Among the exceptional attorneys of Old Natchez were Seargent S. Prentiss, one of antebellum America's most gifted orators; Robert J. Walker, who later served as Secretary of the Treasury and governor of Kansas; Joseph Dunbar Shields, biographer of Seargent S. Prentiss and historian of Old Natchez; and Joseph S. B. Thatcher, who drafted, with the assistance of Horace Mann, Mississippi's first public school statute in 1846.

Since the embroideries of wealth graced the great mansions of Old Natchez, rich planters practiced conspicuous consumption long before the economist Thorstein Veblen coined the phrase. But behind those pillared porticoes, in the drawing rooms and libraries of

Joseph Dunbar Shields, 19th-century Natchez biographer and historian

Robert J. Walker, 19th-century Natchez attorney who served as U.S. Secretary of the Treasury and governor of Kansas

Auburn, Monmouth, Linden and Lansdowne, men of wealth and power often discussed the ideas that separated them or bound them together. And with equal ease many of them discussed great works of literature, Greek dramas, Roman historians and the latest English poets.

Their intellectual curiosity was genuine, and they had the means to indulge it. Some planters, like Stephen Duncan, Adam Louis Bingaman, David Hunt, Haller Nutt and Samuel Boyd, owned extensive libraries. The largest was probably Boyd's library at Arlington, which consisted of 8,000 volumes in more than a dozen languages. William Johnson also owned a large library and subscribed to several periodicals, including *The Saturday Evening Post*, *The New Yorker*, *New York Mirror* and a half dozen newspapers in Mississippi and Louisiana.

Benjamin L.C. Wailes of Natchez and Washington, antebellum Mississippi's best-known man of science, about 1820

Although some of the largest planters and their families shopped in Paris and London, a source of constant complaint among local merchants, Natchez was a significant marketplace in Southwest Mississippi. Its retail businesses included small specialty shops and large general mercantile stores.

Records show that in 1833 Miss L. Dowell operated a "glassware, china and crockery" shop, and Emile Profilet owned a store which sold jewelry and watches. Like their modern counterparts, some shop-keepers of Old Natchez were forced to liquidate or cut prices to reduce their inventories. An 1854 advertisement in a local newspaper reads: "THE EXCITEMENT CONTINUES! REDUCED PRICES on French linens, embroideries, organdies and other summer items."

As would be expected in a town where the Code Duello was an honored tradition, there were several gun shops in Natchez, with Stephen Odell owning the largest one.

In 1852 the Natchez Building Association was established "to accumulate savings funds and award loans for the building or buying of houses." That early form of a savings and loan institution may have been the only one of its kind in the South. Chartered by Ralph North and

An advertisement for guns from the shop of S. Odell, corner of Commerce and Main streets in Natchez, about 1853

Giles Hillyer, it charged six percent on its loans. Mississippi's largest insurance company, the Natchez Protection Insurance Company, one of the state's few textile mills, and one of its largest timber mills were also located in Natchez.

Other large business activity included a timber mill owned by Andrew Brown. Located at the north end of the landing under the hill, it was a highly profitable industry. Brown was the only Natchez nabob who lived below the bluffs. His mansion, Magnolia Vale, with its majestic magnolias and 15-acre botanical garden, was a showplace of Old Natchez. But with the widening river lapping at its gardens, the house was finally destroyed by fire in 1947, only to be rebuilt in exactly its same position.

Fires, epidemics and natural disasters were the bane of Southern cities, and Natchez suffered from all three,

Magnolia Vale, home of wealthy lumberman Andrew Brown, with some of its renowned gardens, in a 1900 photograph

though not as much as many other towns its size. In 1847 Natchez had three volunteer fire companies, four full-time firemen and a state-supported hospital. A private relief agency, the Natchez Charitable Association, was established in the early 1850s.

The worst natural disaster Natchez experienced in the years before the Civil War was the tornado of 1840, which caused $5 million in property damage and left 300 dead and 600 seriously injured. A steamboat at the landing, set adrift during the storm, was found two weeks later, 150 miles downriver with 51 bodies on board.

Although many major religious denominations established churches in Old Natchez, the town was not extremely religious.

Lorenzo Dow, an eccentric circuit rider who planted

Methodism in the Natchez region, wrote in his 1815 journal that he doubted if there were "three Christians in the town, either black or white."

Presbyterians, who sent missionaries to Natchez in 1800, had a congregation of 49 in 1824 and a congregation of 135 in 1837. Optimistic members built First Presbyterian Church to seat 700 in the late 1820s.

Trinity Episcopal Church was organized, it is said, at Stephen Duncan's home, in order to provide an appropriate setting for the wedding of local gentleman's daughter. Trinity's original building, the oldest church building in Natchez still in use, was begun in 1822 and completed in 1823. It, too, looked to the future with a seating capacity of 600.

At the urging of the Roman Catholic Society of Natchez, Pope Gregory XVI established the Diocese of Natchez in 1837. St. Mary's Cathedral, the first Diocesan Cathedral of Catholicism in Mississippi, was completed in 1854.

Baptists also established their first congregation in Natchez in 1837. Despite all this religious activity, a major 20th-century historian of Old Natchez, D. Clayton

First Presbyterian Church on South Pearl Street, about 1909

Artist's rendering of Trinity Episcopal Church on South Commerce Street, about 1830, quite different from the rendering by John James Audubon in his 1822 Natchez landscape

Jefferson Street Methodist Church, about 1880

James, found that only 15 percent of the white population maintained church affiliation in 1815. By 1860, James said, that percentage had increased only slightly to 28 percent.

It was politics rather than theology, the here-and-now, not the hereafter, that stirred and riled the white men of Old Natchez. In antebellum Mississippi, and especially in Natchez, the parallel lines of party and class divided the Whigs from the Democrats, the nabobs from the nobodies, embittering their dialogue throughout the 1830s and 1840s. But in the 1850s, with an increasing Northern agitation for the abolition of slavery, the Southern Whigs and Democrats made an uneasy truce. They did not settle their differences; they sublimated them. They closed ranks to defend a labor system that had become by then the living symbol of the Southern way of life.

St. Mary's (Catholic) Cathedral on the corner of Main and Union streets, about 1890

Chapter 5

The Great Planters of Natchez

Approximately 60 families in Natchez and Adams County achieved the luxury of great wealth in the mid-19th century. The makers of those fortunes were not born to the manor because there was no native American aristocracy and few, if any, of the English nobility moved to the colonies. Among the first generation of the Natchez gentry were former Spanish and English officials who received large land grants for various services they rendered to their governments. Others were enterprising merchants, lawyers, physicians and land speculators who sank their surplus capital into land and slaves, which ultimately became the source of Southern wealth and status.

Among the first generation, and until the cotton boom of the 1830s, social and class lines were fluid, and upward mobility was common. But among the second and third generation of Natchez aristocrats, social and class distinctions were more fixed and much less flexible. To these people, kinship and bloodlines were as important as wealth. Indeed, these privileged people loaned each other money when the unfortunate or careless among them was in need.

The lure of the gentry's leisured lifestyle had a compelling effect on Southern whites. Planters and their families often flaunted their wealth, inciting the ire of common folk and exciting their envy. Although only 1 percent of Southern whites ever belonged to that exclusive elite, the enduring Southern dream was to own land and slaves and to become a great planter.

On the eve of the Civil War, a Mississippi editor explained and defended the Southern way of life. "A large plantation and Negroes are the *ultima thule* of every

Southern gentleman's ambition," he wrote. To achieve that goal, he continued, "the lawyer pores over his dusty tomes, the merchant measures his tape, the doctor rolls his pills, the editor drives his quill and the mechanic his plane." Every Southern male, he concluded, "is thus trained from infancy to think and prepare for the attainment of this end."

From the outside, the lives of great planters appeared easy; they seemed to prosper without effort. But the prominent planters of Natchez, as the following biographical sketches show, were not idle aristocrats who whiled away their time in the lengthening shadows of summer. Successful planters were also successful businessmen. They were men of wealth, but they were also men of energy and ambition. Planters operated large enterprises that required leadership skills, complex accounting and production procedures, good land management and an intricate knowledge of human relations. Any planter who neglected his fields for horse races or other pleasures soon regretted it. There was a saying in the Old South, "There is no fertilizer like the footsteps of the master."

The following sketches highlight a few of the most interesting and most enterprising of the great planters of Natchez.

ADAM LOUIS BINGAMAN

Born into one of the Old South's wealthiest networks of families which included the Surgets, Lintots, Minors, Dunbars, Hutchinses, Vousdans, Chotards and Wilkinses, Adam Louis Bingaman inherited seven separate estates. "Gifted by nature in mind and personal appearance," as one biographer put it, he was graduated at the head of his class at Harvard. The young Bingaman was known as the *jeunesse doree*, the "golden youth" of the river. As the master of Fatherland Plantation and the owner of 310 slaves, he was a second-generation aristocrat whose "energies were largely absorbed by sport and politics." His fame as a horse breeder, the success of his thoroughbreds at the track and his love for the sport of kings led the New Orleans *Picayune* to dub him "Napoleon of the Turf." As a politician he held the distinction of being one of the very few men to have chaired both houses of the Mississippi state legislature, serving as both Speaker of the House of Representatives and President of the Senate.

Adam Louis Bingaman, the aristocratic "golden youth" of the Mississippi River

A popular Whig in a Democratic state, Bingaman was a brilliant conversationalist, learned, well-read, multilingual and a popular dinner guest. The historian J. F. H. Claiborne describes a dinner party honoring Edward Everette, the esteemed Massachusetts lawyer and vice-presidential candidate, on the eve of his departure from Natchez. The dinner was at Sunnyside, Samuel Davis's estate. Everette gave a late-night soliloquy, quoting from the Spanish writer Cervantes in the original. When Bingaman was called upon to reply, he responded in a language which guests soon realized was a Choctaw dialect. Bingaman, who had married a woman from Massachusetts, spoke: "Mingo of the Massachusetts, farewell!! Return to the wigwam of your fathers, where the great water rolls its billows and the voice of the Great Spirit thunders along the shores. Tell them you have seen the Great River," he continued, "and that in every hamlet on its banks you have found men of the Massa-

Lexington, a famous Natchez race horse, in an 1853 painting

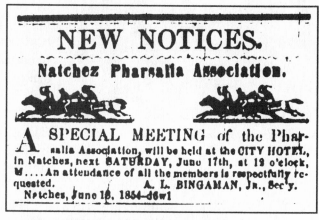

An 1854 notice of a meeting of the Pharsalia Association, a group of Natchez horse-racing enthusiasts

chusetts tribe, wedded to the daughters of the land, prosperous and happy. Sachem! May sunshine light your path." After Bingaman's plantation holdings declined through bad luck and poor management and after his wife died, Bingaman and his black mistress moved to New Orleans, where they remained until his death in 1869. The William Johnson papers, which contain Johnson's diary and family letters, also include several letters from Bingaman to Johnson's children after Bingaman moved to New Orleans. Bingaman was Johnson's closest white associate, and his letters to Johnson's children reflect a deep friendship and concern for them. Bingaman's daughter by his mistress remained in New Orleans until her death in 1937.

STEPHEN DUNCAN

Stephen Duncan of Auburn, vast land holder, planter and businessman

After completing his medical studies at Dickinson College, Stephen Duncan left his native Pennsylvania in 1808, arriving in Natchez to practice medicine and to seek his fortune. Soon after his arrival, he married Margaret Ellis, and after her death four years later, he married Catherine Bingaman. Both of his wives belonged to old and wealthy Natchez families. Through those marital alliances, by which he obtained large land holdings, and by what one historian calls "his uncommon entrepreneurial skills," Stephen Duncan amassed one of the vast fortunes of the Old South.

Like many of his planter peers, Duncan diversified his holdings to include both cotton and sugar plantations, banking interests, stocks, securities and other commercial interests in Mississippi, Louisiana, New York and Pennsylvania. At the height of his affluence in 1850, Duncan was the largest individual cotton producer and slave holder in the world. He owned eight plantations, more than 1,000 slaves and was producing more than 4,000 bales of cotton annually. His total wealth was estimated to be in excess of $2 million.

In 1827 Duncan purchased Auburn, one of the grand houses of Old Natchez, which was designed and built by Levi Weeks. At the mansion Duncan kept a staff of 23 domestic slaves. Among the many famous guests at Auburn were Henry Clay; Edward Everette Hale, author of "The Man Without a Country"; and John Howard Payne, songster and playwright who penned the ever-popular "Home, Sweet Home." Duncan and Adam Bingaman, his wife's brother, often dined together at Auburn and discussed literature and horse racing, two of the many passions they held in common. Duncan, like Bingaman, was an ardent Whig who dabbled in local and

Auburn, designed and built by Levi Weeks, in a 1940 photograph

state politics. He was a delegate to the Mississippi Constitutional Convention of 1832 and was a member of the Natchez Junto, the closest thing to a political machine in antebellum Mississippi.

In 1831 Duncan took the lead in establishing the Mississippi Colonization Society. He contributed to it financially and held office in both the state and national organizations. He spent 12 years trying to implement Isaac Ross's will, manumitting his slaves and returning them to Africa. His commitment and continued support for that unpopular cause cost him dearly in public esteem and personal friendships. Duncan never did become truly Southern philosophically or temperamentally. He was troubled by the moral aspects of slavery; he was a nationalist rather than a states' rightist; and he vehemently opposed secession and Civil War. After the Civil War began Duncan gave no support to the Confederate States of America, either moral or financial. He invested in northern railroads and in public land in the Western territories rather than in Confederate securities. In 1863 Duncan left Natchez for New York, where he remained until his death in 1867. In 1911, Duncan family heirs donated Auburn and its spacious grounds to the City of Natchez for a recreational park.

WILLIAM ST. JOHN ELLIOTT

Unlike some Natchez planters, unrenowned for their piety, William St. John Elliott was very active in local church affairs. He was a strong supporter and financial contributor to the Natchez Roman Catholic Society and greeted the news of the establishment of the Natchez Diocese in 1837 with warm enthusiasm. But like the other great planters of Natchez, Elliott also had commercial and business interests. He was one of the founders and served for many years as president of the Natchez Protection Insurance Company. Also a livestock breeder, his fine herd of Ayrshire dairy cattle supplied fresh milk for his plantation slaves and his family.

Elliott, a Whig, was an intimate friend of Henry Clay.

When Clay visited Natchez in 1842, Elliott gave a grand reception at his newly completed mansion, D'Evereux, one of the most imposing landmarks in a town of many monuments. It is believed that on his visit to D'Evereux in 1842 an unusually fine portrait of Clay was painted by a French artist.

In at least one way, Elliott could have been an inspiration for one of William Faulkner's most famous characters. In his masterpiece, *Absalom! Absalom!*, Faulkner creates a character named Thomas Sutpen, a Southern planter with no legitimate male heir. In that convoluted story, Faulkner shows how possessing and compelling was the urge for continuity among Southern planters, the need to have sons to leave their land to and to carry on their bloodline.

William St. John Elliott, a wealthy Natchez planter who entertained Henry Clay several times in his home, D'Evereux

D'Evereux, home of William St. John Elliott

Henry Clay in an 1842 portrait which is thought to have been painted at the Natchez mansion D'Evereux

Elliott married Anne Conner of Second Creek, a woman twice widowed who brought to the marriage two large estates. But the couple had no sons. As the years passed, the pain of having no sons to carry on and rule over his holdings preyed upon Elliott's mind. He hatched a scheme: upon his death, Elliott would will D'Evereux and his other holdings to his wife for the remainder of her life. Upon her death, his estate, including D'Evereux, would go to a nephew, provided the nephew legally changed his name to William St. John Elliott II, "so as to represent me as my son," Elliott wrote. If the boy refused to accept the condition of his bequest, according to one version of the story, D'Evereux would go to the Natchez Diocese for use as a Catholic home for orphaned boys. The parents of the nephew, who was a minor, declined the bequest on behalf of their son. After the boy's parents refused to accept the condition of Elliott's will, Anne Elliott provided an alternate nearby site for the orphanage, called D'Evereux Hall, and contributed additional

D'Evereux Hall Orphan Asylum, established on land near the mansion D'Evereux, in an 1890 drawing

funds for its construction. By that arrangement, as the story goes, she was able to keep the mansion D'Evereux in her family. Upon her death in 1876, she willed the mansion to a favorite niece.

ALVAREZ FISK

Although he owned several large plantations, Alvarez Fisk devoted his personal attention to his various commercial holdings. In addition to his planting interests, Fisk was one of the state's largest cotton commissioners. He owned a brokerage house in New Orleans and several mercantile establishments in Natchez and was an investor in the Natchez Steam Packet Company. His total worth in 1833 was estimated at $600,000, but by the time of his death in 1853, it was considerably more. Rather than live in the country on one of his plantations, Fisk preferred to live in Natchez at his mansion, Choctaw, which he purchased about 1840. His extensive plantation holdings afforded him membership in the Natchez aristocracy, even though he was a Bostonian by birth and a lawyer by profession. He was a Whig, like most other planters along Second Creek, and a strong financial backer of the Natchez Junto. He also made large donations to religious and philanthropic enterprises.

Fisk is best remembered as the father of the Natchez Institute, the first public school in Natchez. For several years during the early 1840s, Fisk was the most active member of a small group of citizens who promoted the cause of public education. Among that group

Alvarez Fisk, a wealthy Natchez planter who was one of Mississippi's largest cotton commissioners

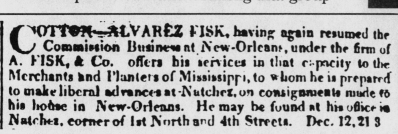

An 1825 advertisement for Alverez Fisk's firm

93

were Charles L. Dubisson, former president of Jefferson College; John Anthony Quitman, future governor of the state; and Judge J. S. B. Thatcher, a member of the state Supreme Court. In 1845 Fisk donated the site on which the first public school house in Natchez was built. A few years later, after a burgeoning enrollment had outgrown the existing structure, Fisk donated the funds for a new brick building. Although there was some opposition from several property owners, the town council established a school tax of three and one-half mills and decreed that a substantial portion of the town's annual revenue would go to the Institute. The year after the Natchez Institute was founded, Mississippi established a state system of public education, thus providing some state funding for Natchez schools.

Fisk also promoted the establishment of a state university at Natchez, which would have included schools of liberal arts, law and medicine. But his effort in that

The Natchez Institute, Natchez's first public school, established on land donated in 1845 by Alverez Fisk, in an 1890 photograph

regard was to no avail. Fisk did not live long enough to witness Southern secession or the devastation that followed. The commercial fortune which he had accumulated was lost in the aftermath of the war.

DAVID HUNT

From his uncle, Abijah Hunt, who was killed in 1811 in a duel with George Poindexter, David Hunt inherited a chain of gins and mercantile establishments. He also inherited nearly 4,000 acres of land. Hunt gradually converted most of his business assets into land and slaves, amassing a large fortune. Before dividing his holdings among his seven children, David Hunt owned, according to one source, almost 2,000 slaves and 26 plantations. He had a house in Natchez but spent most of his time in the countryside at Woodlawn, near Cole's Creek. Before the division of his assets, which also included railroad interests and real estate in Ohio, Hunt's combined wealth was more than $2 million.

David Hunt, owner of 2,000 slaves and 26 Natchez-area plantations

Among the wealthiest men in the Old South, Hunt was considered by B. L. C. Wailes as a "model planter." Most of Hunt's plantations, like Henry Clay's Ashland Plantation, were self-sufficient enterprises which not only produced their own food supplies but also manufactured most of the farming implements necessary for the production of cotton. In 1860, at the age of 82, Hunt owned 468 slaves and more than 12,000 acres, 2,500 of which were improved land.

Hunt was generous with his vast wealth and made substantial gifts to the American and Mississippi Colonization Societies. He was a founder and an officeholder in the Mississippi chapter of the Colonization Society. Over his lifetime he donated approximately $150,000 to Oakland College, near Natchez. In recognition of his support for religious and educational endeavors, Mississippi Presbyterians named a boys' preparatory school near Port Gibson in his honor as well as in the honor of Jeremiah Chamberlain, the first president of Oakland College. They called the school Chamberlain-Hunt.

Three mansions, built on land owned by David Hunt: Lansdowne, top, in a 1950 photograph; Oakwood, center, in a 1900 photograph; and Homewood, in a 1938 photograph

At the approach of the Civil War, Hunt's children urged him to dispose of his Northern holdings, but he refused to do so. He told his children, and anyone else who would listen, that the impending Civil War would be long and bloody and economically devastating to the South. Of his Northern property, he said to his children, "Someday it may be our asylum."

LEVIN R. MARSHALL

Levin R. Marshall was linked by marriage to the Chotard family and the Duncan clan. One of his sons, George, married a daughter of wealthy planter David Hunt, and the couple built Lansdowne on a portion of the Hunt family property. Marshall's family connections, plus his own personal wealth which included 817 slaves, 24,000 acres of land and one of the largest livestock herds in Southwest Mississippi, placed him in the upper echelons of the Natchez elite. The Marshall family lived with 32 house slaves in Natchez at Richmond, a large mansion with three distinct sections and three different architectural styles.

Levin R. Marshall, extremely successful Natchez planter, banker and land owner

Richmond, home of Levin R. Marshall, built in three distinct periods of history, in a 1935 photograph

As a member of a syndicate which included several other Natchez planters and businessmen, Marshall owned vast land holdings in Arkansas and Texas, most of which was purchased for speculation. Marshall's business and commercial interests in the North were also quite extensive. He was president of the Commercial Bank of Natchez and at one time owned the famous Mansion House hotel. An officer and stockholder in the Natchez Steam Packet Company, he was one of the largest stockholders in the Natchez Protection Insurance Company. In return for his financial backing of Sam Houston and the Texas Revolution, Marshall received a large land grant in Texas. The town of Marshall, Texas, was later established on the site of the land grant and is supposedly named after Levin Marshall.

When Jenny Lind came to Natchez in February 1851, so the story goes in Natchez lore, a winter storm had iced the city streets. Her stage managers were unable to get her piano from the Natchez landing up the slippery slope of Silver Street. To the great relief of the promoters of the concert, Levin Marshall allowed the use of his family's grand piano at Richmond; it was moved to the Methodist Church, where the performance was held. According to another version of the Jenny Lind story, the Marshalls' piano was used for the concert because it had the best sound of any piano in Natchez.

Whatever the case about the visiting singer's piano, Levin Marshall was an outspoken Unionist whose Poplar Grove Plantation was pillaged during the Civil War by Confederate raiders. Eventually, Marshall left Natchez and moved to New York, where he had substantial commercial interests.

THE MINORS

Stephen Minor was a colonial planter and patriarch of a famous and wealthy Natchez family. He came to Natchez from Pennsylvania in 1780 and fought with the Spanish troops against the British at Mobile and Pensacola. His marksmanship and gallantry impressed

Don Estevan Minor, acting governor of Natchez in 1798

The "Yellow Duchess," Catherine Lintot Minor, wife of Don Estevan Minor

the Spaniards, who granted him a large tract of Natchez-area land and appointed him deputy governor of Spanish Natchez. He was closely associated with Gov. Manuel Gayoso and served as acting governor of Natchez in 1798 after Gayoso moved to New Orleans.

Known as Don Estevan among the Spaniards, Stephen Minor endeared himself to the new American government and to the new American settlers by his friendly cooperation during the transfer of Natchez from Spain to the United States. Minor remained in Natchez and became both wealthy and popular. He married the daughter of John Ellis, the prosperous planter of White Cliffs. Minor is associated with the house Airlie, which he built about 1794, and later with Concord, a mansion made famous by Manuel Gayoso.

Claiborne described Stephen Minor as an extremely hospitable and opulent planter who "lived in elegant style." Minor's third wife, Catherine Lintot Minor, is known in Natchez folklore as the "Yellow Duchess." The origin of the "Legend of the Yellow Duchess" remains a mystery, though direct family descendants in 1991 attested to its accuracy. The first recorded version of the story is found in one of Harnett T. Kane's books on Natchez. According to Kane's account, Catherine Lintot Minor was so enchanted by the color yellow that she enveloped herself in it. Every dress she wore was yellow, as was her entire ensemble down to the feather in her hat. She entertained her guests in a drawing room that "glimmered with yellow walls, yellow carpets on the floor, mirrors and cornices of gold, sofas and chairs to match, mantel of tawny shade," Kane wrote. Craftsmen installed golden cloth in her yellow coach; she searched until she found four horses of golden hue, and even her house servants were mulattoes of yellow tint. The "Yellow Duchess" and Don Estevan lived happily at Concord, where five of their children were born. Two sons, William and John, followed in the footsteps of their illustrious father and also became great planters. William spent his autumns and winters at Concord, which he inherited, and spent his summers in the Louisiana "Sugar Bowl," where he owned several sugar plantations. He was a sportsman whose thoroughbreds matched those of Adam Bingaman. He also introduced cricket as an organized sport in the Old Southwest and was a leader in the founding of the Natchez Cricket Club. John Minor, his brother, lived at another Natchez mansion, Oakland. He enlarged his inheritance and by 1860 had an estimated worth of $555,600.

HALLER NUTT

The son of Dr. Rush Nutt, who developed the highly successful Petit Gulf cotton seed, Dr. Haller Nutt also perfected a new strain of cotton in 1841, known as Egypto-Mexican. The new strain was superior to the Petit Gulf variety and was adopted by many planters in the Old Southwest. Haller Nutt, a much more prosperous and extensive planter than his father, accumulated a

Top left, Haller Nutt, scientist who developed the Egypto-Mexican variety of cotton and became a prosperous planter; top right, design for Longwood by Philadelphia architect Samuel Sloan, about 1852; and, above, Longwood, Haller Nutt's uncompleted dream house, begun in 1860, in a 1940 photograph.

PRICES IN 1850 - 1855

Land per acre $100
Slaves (field hand) $1,500
Cotton seed per bushel ....$1.50-$2.50
Steam engine, to run cotton gin $1,450
Mississippi State Hospital, Natchez
  First class patients per day $3
  With private nurse $5
Oats per bushel.. $.80
Bacon per pound... $.08
Oysters per hundred $1
Haircut... $.25 (2 bits)
Shave .... $.125 (1 bit)
Natchez mayor's annual salary $575
Annual subscription rates for newspapers and journals
  Natchez Daily Courier $8
  Illustrated London News $10
  Saturday Evening Post $2
  Godey's Lady's Book $3
Wildwood Springs resort hotel per month $30
  (23 miles from Natchez)

sizable fortune by the time of the Civil War. In 1860 Haller Nutt owned 21 plantations in Louisiana and Mississippi, 800 slaves and 40,000 acres of land. He estimated his net income at $228,370.

That same year Nutt began the construction of his home, Longwood, one of the most unusual and most recognizable buildings in the South. He employed a Philadelphia architect, Samuel Sloan, to design and supervise the construction of this six-story, octagonal mansion, which was crowned by a Byzantine dome featuring 16 clerestory windows. The architectural innovations of Longwood, especially the highly advanced lighting and ventilation systems, more than matched its grandiosity. One of its 32 rooms was to be a library, designed to house 10,000 volumes. Longwood's spacious grounds included a 20-acre rose garden with 500 varieties of roses. It was said that Mrs. Nutt had to take a carriage to pick roses.

When the Civil War began in 1861, craftsmen whom Samuel Sloan had brought to Longwood from Pennsylvania fled from the South back home, unknowingly suspending forever the completion of Longwood. In 1861 the building was half-finished; the Nutt family was forced to occupy the only completed floor, the basement. For more than a century they resided there. Today, Longwood remains unfinished and is one of Natchez's major tourist attractions. In the words of the poet Matthew Arnold, the house has become a monument "that whispers the last enchantments" of an earlier age.

JOHN ANTHONY QUITMAN

Like many other Southern statesmen, John Anthony Quitman justified slavery and the plantation system on the grounds that it produced a learned class of leadership with the leisure to prepare itself for public service. Quitman soon realized, however, that no matter how firm his beliefs, Natchez aristocrats would not turn over their vast holdings to virtual strangers, even if they were married to their daughters. In 1824, only three years after coming to Natchez, Quitman married Eliza Turner, the daughter of Henry Turner and the niece of Judge Edward Turner, both of whom were planters with large commercial interests. Before the marriage, Quitman was required to sign a prenuptial agreement which included the statement: "said land and Negroes...shall go to the Heirs and personal representatives of the said Eliza Turner, and not to the Heirs and personal representatives of said John Anthony Quitman." After Quitman acquired the imposing Natchez mansion Monmouth and achieved military and political prominence, he was accepted into the Turner family and the Natchez aristocracy. Using his Natchez connections and his reputation as a leading attorney, Quitman launched a highly successful political and military career. Claiborne wrote that Quitman was "greedy for military fame" and that "a more ambitious man never lived." After serving in the state legislature and on the state appeals court, Quitman received a temporary appointment as brigadier general in the United States Army and became a national hero in the Mexican War. During America's brief occupation of

John A. Quitman, Mississippi governor, U.S. congressman, Mexican War hero and noted attorney

Mexico in 1847-1848, Quitman was provisional governor of Mexico City. His military exploits in the Mexican War made him a contender for the vice-presidential nomination in 1848, but his first love was the military, and Quitman sought a permanent commission in the regular army. After failing to secure the military appointment, Quitman ran for and was overwhelmingly elected governor of Mississippi in 1849. While serving as governor, Quitman was invited by the Cuban revolutionary movement to lead its army in revolt against Spain. Quitman had long been a supporter of the Cuban insurgency and had backed the movement in violation of American neutrality laws. He declined the offer

Monmouth, home of John Anthony Quitman, in an early 20th-century photograph

from the Cuban insurgents in 1851 because he believed that the slave states would soon secede and his services would be needed in the war for Southern independence which secession would undoubtedly precipitate.

In 1855 Quitman was elected to the U.S. Congress, where he served until his death in 1858. Quitman was unusual among the great planters of Natchez. He was a Democrat, an ardent secessionist and a supporter of the establishment of an independent Southern confederacy. It is quite possible that Quitman's greed for military fame overrode the interests of property which caused most other wealthy planters to reject secession as a radical and unpredictable solution to their problems with the North.

STANTON FAMILY

By the 1850s there were several branches of the Stanton family in the Natchez area. Their extensive holdings in Adams County and in Louisiana made them one of the wealthiest clans in Natchez. Like most other prominent members of the Natchez aristocracy, the Stantons were linked by marriage to several other elite families, including the family of Gerard Brandon, Mississippi's first native-born governor.

Shortly after coming to Natchez from Belfast, Ireland, Frederick Stanton established a lucrative cotton commission business in partnership with Aylette Buckner. On his way up the financial and social scale, Stanton purchased Cherokee, a downtown Natchez home. At the zenith of his wealth, in the 1850s, he built magnificent Stanton Hall, where he kept 17 house slaves. Just prior to the Civil War, Frederick Stanton owned 444 slaves, 15,109 acres of land and six plantations.

Frederick Stanton's brother, David Stanton, owned another large downtown home, The Elms, and was also a cotton merchant as well as a planter. William Stanton, still another member of

Frederick Stanton, Natchez planter and cotton broker

*Stanton Hall, built in the late 1850s,
in a 1940 photograph*

the Stanton clan, owned Windy Hill Manor, a mansion
made famous by Aaron Burr, who stayed there while he
was in Natchez in 1807.

THE SURGETS

One of the most extensive and interesting of the
planter kingdoms of Old Natchez was the province of the
golden Surgets. The patriarch was Pierre Surget, a former
French sea captain who some say was a pirate of the
Spanish main. For his services to the Spanish crown, he
received a land grant of 2,500 acres near Natchez, where
he built Cherry Grove in 1788. After his death in 1796
his enterprising New Jersey wife, Catherine, enlarged the
Surget holdings and left their sons and daughters about
7,000 acres when she died in 1805. One son, Jacob,

maintained ownership of an Adams County plantation but moved to New York.

Francis, another son, extended the Surget holdings and acquired vast stretches of land, including 50,000 acres in Arkansas. He was a 4,000-bale-a-year planter with 8,000 acres of cotton and sugar land in cultivation in Mississippi and Louisiana. Claiborne said Francis Surget "was the most extensive and successful planter Mississippi had ever seen." An Arkansas newspaper was not so complimentary. The editor referred to Surget as "a nabob from Natchez" and derided him for being as "rich as Croesus" and an absentee land owner. At the time of his death in the mid-1850s, Francis Surget's estate, which included railroad securities and other commercial interests, was valued at well over $2 million. Most of his estate went to his son, Francis II, called Frank.

Francis Surget, a 4,000-bale-a-year Natchez planter

Frank and his wife, Charlotte Linton Surget, purchased the palatial home Clifton from Charlotte's mother, Anna Maria Bingaman Linton. Clifton was located near the edge of the Natchez bluff, with a commanding view of the Great River. During the Civil War, Frank traded extensively with both Confederates and with Federals and often entertained Union officers at his home on the bluff. According to a Natchez legend, the Union officer in charge of local fortifications was offended because he had not been invited to a grand party at Clifton. Soon after the slight occurred, the fortifications officer decided to build a gun placement on the Natchez bluff to give the Federals more effective control of the river. In drawing the plans for an earthwork fortification, the officer is supposed to have exacted revenge by routing the earthworks right through the site of Clifton and ordering the demolition of Frank Surget's magnificent mansion. For whatever reason, personal affront or military necessity, Clifton was summarily demolished and a large earthwork fortification, known as Fort McPherson, was constructed in the old northern suburbs of the city. Within the earthwork boundary were several of the great

Jacob Surget, planter who left Natchez for New York

James Surget, owner of nine Natchez-area plantations and 453 slaves

Natchez houses: Airlie, The Towers, Riverview, The Wigwam, The Burn and Cottage Gardens.

Pierre Surget's third son, James, also multiplied his inheritance through wise purchases and marital alliances. James kept Cherry Grove and 16 house slaves to serve his family's needs. Owner of nine plantations and 453 slaves, James, with his brother Frank, controlled almost 100,000 acres of land. His son, James Jr., was said to have inherited from his father and other Surget family members more than 1,000 slaves.

All the Surgets, like most other Natchez aristocrats, kept within a small circumference of friends and families, determined to hold on to what was theirs, either by industry or by inheritance. Their love of the land and their way of life, and their struggle to keep them both in the aftermath of the Civil War, is another chapter in the history of the great planters of Natchez.

Arlington, early 19th-century home of Jane Surget White, daughter of Pierre Surget, the great Natchez land baron

Chapter 6
The Civil War

On the eve of the American Civil War, Gov. John J. Pettus told the people of Mississippi that we "must go down into Egypt while Herod rules in Judea." Mississippians followed Pettus out of the Union and down into Egypt. But when they returned from their perilous and self-imposed exile, they found a New Jerusalem. The world that they had known was remade by the Civil War. Freedmen described the new order by saying, "The bottom rail is now on top."

Natchez and Adams County were reluctant followers of Pettus. Many wealthy planters and merchants, like Stephen Duncan, Haller Nutt and the Surgets, were loathe to leave the Union. Indeed, some never embraced the Confederacy. Others, like Samuel Boyd, Charles Dahlgren and the Metcalfes, gave full allegiance to the Cotton Republic, as it was sometimes called.

Adams County's two delegates to the 1861 Secession Convention, Alexander K. Farrar and Josiah Winchester, were typical of the county's divided loyalties. Both went as anti-secession delegates to the state convention. However, once war was inevitable, Farrar enlisted in the army of the Confederacy and served throughout the war. Winchester, on the other hand, refused to give any aid or comfort to the rebellion and cooperated with federal military authorities during the occupation of Natchez.

The town's two newspapers were also divided, one for secession and one against. The *Courier,* edited by Giles M. Hillyer, was strongly Union; the *Natchez Free Trader,* edited by William Wood, was just as strongly in favor of secession.

After the establishment of the Confederate States of America on February 4, 1861, and especially after the firing on Fort Sumter on April 12, 1861, most Natchez citizens gave allegiance to the new Southern nation. Fourteen military units were formed in Natchez in the early months of the war, and approximately 1,500 soldiers, more than half of the city's white population, were enrolled in the Confederate Army. A home guard unit of about 75 men beyond the draft age was also established. Known as the Silver Greys, they were commanded by Capt. H. B. Shaw.

As each military unit left Natchez, it was feted and saluted. Parades were an almost daily diversion in the first few months of the war. During this heady time, even the Unionist editor of the Natchez *Courier* boasted that Adams County contributed almost as many squads as Warren County, even though Warren's white population was three times that of Adams'.

Southerners who had not supported secession now supported the Confederate nation which their fathers and sons were pledged to defend and die for. For them, the struggle had reached a new level, a higher plane. The rebellion had become a war for Southern independence, and they likened themselves to the American patriots who gained their freedom from England by revolution. That change in public sentiment was noted by a London *Times* correspondent who visited Natchez in June 1861. He reported that a large majority of the city's population was by then in favor of the Confederacy.

Confederate Gen. William Thompson Martin of Natchez, in an 1880 portrait

One of the best illustrations of that dramatic shift in sentiment is William T. Martin, owner of a large home in Natchez called Montaigne. Martin had been an ardent and adamant opponent of secession, but after the Southern Confederacy was established, he declared his willingness "to fight to sustain it." At the outbreak of the war, Martin enrolled in the army of the Confederacy as a captain, along with his Adams Troop of cavalry. His military daring and command skills, admirable if not necessary traits of a good cavalry officer, won him quick promotions and larger commands. At war's end Martin was a major general and a division commander.

Montaigne, the home of Confederate Gen. William T. Martin, in a 1920 photograph

Opposition to the Civil War among large Natchez planters and merchants was not rooted exclusively in their own self-interest, although they certainly had the most to lose. Realizing that an agrarian society could not successfully make war against an industrial nation, they were among the very few Southerners who predicted a long and bloody war that would ultimately ruin the South economically and would inevitably lead to the abolition of slavery.

The control of the Mississippi River was an imperative for both sides in the American Civil War. In a complex campaign designed to capture and control the river, Union naval forces under Adm. David Farragut launched an attack against New Orleans, while a Union fleet under Adm. David Porter moved downriver from Cairo, Illinois, against Memphis. While those naval engagements were taking place, a massive land force under Gen. U. S. Grant was moving southwestward through Tennessee toward Vicksburg, which became his ultimate objective. Farragut, coming upriver from New Orleans, and Porter, downriver from Memphis, planned to rendezvous with Grant at Vicksburg. Known as the "Gibraltar of the Confederacy," Vicksburg was located on a loess bluff high above a sharp bend in the Great River. Both the people of the South and the Confederate command structure believed Vicksburg was an impregnable fortress which could not be taken.

Confederate military strategy and tactics were limited by the South's defensive posture, and the Confederate Army's most viable option was to concentrate its forces on disrupting, obstructing and ultimately preventing Grant from reaching Vicksburg by land. That strategy left

U.S. Gen. Ulysses S. Grant, who visited Natchez in 1863

U.S. Adm. David G. Farragut of the USS Hartford, in an 1863 portrait

Dunleith, home of Confederate Brig. Gen. Charles Dahlgren, in a 1940 photograph

the small towns along the southern stretches of the Mississippi River exposed and vulnerable to Union gunboats.

Brig. Gen. Charles Dahlgren, owner of the imposing Natchez mansion Dunleith and commander of a small Confederate force assigned to defend the Mississippi Gulf

Coast, complained to Gen. P. G. T. Beauregard that Natchez was left defenseless. Beauregard expressed his regret that the Confederacy could not adequately defend "important cities" like Natchez but explained to Dahlgren that the South's best hope was to "throw all our forces into large armies" and win some important victory over the Union army to gain diplomatic recognition and financial aid from Europe.

Confederate foreign policy was based almost exclusively on "cotton diplomacy." The Southern strategy was to withhold cotton from the European market in an effort to force England and France to extend diplomatic recognition and provide financial support for the Confederate States. Because cotton diplomacy would succeed only if the cotton supply was short, a corollary to that policy was the decrease in cotton production and an increase in grains and other food crops. Newspapers loyal to the Confederate cause touted the advantages of "King Corn" and questioned the patriotism of planters who did not embrace a varied husbandry. Cotton diplomacy failed because an unforeseen surplus in the world's cotton supply was more than adequate in the 1860s to keep English textile mills humming.

Along with the first dispatches from the Battle of Shiloh on April 6-7, 1862, came word that several members of the Natchez Southrons had been killed and wounded in that bloody battle. More bad news arrived on April 29. Adm. Farragut's saltwater fleet had captured New Orleans, and his gunboats were steaming upriver.

The war finally reached Natchez on the afternoon of May 12, 1862, when James S. Palmer, commander of the *USS Iroquois*, docked at the Natchez landing and sent a letter to Mayor John Hunter demanding the surrender of Natchez. The next day Hunter surrendered the town and issued a proclamation calling on the people to keep the peace. Two weeks later Farragut and his flagship *Hartford* anchored off Natchez.

Gen. Charles Dahlgren had been in Natchez the day

before the surrender with a small command of 14 troops and 100 unarmed Virginia recruits. Also under his authority were a number of conscripts, but he complained bitterly that they "would not do duty" in defense of Natchez. As the Federals approached Natchez, Dahlgren withdrew from the city and issued an order to burn all cotton within 10 miles of the river or to remove it beyond that distance.

The general also reported to his superiors that a Natchez minister had refused to pray for President Jefferson Davis, an act considered treasonous. Dahlgren asked if the minister should be imprisoned. The Confederate high command told Dahlgren not to arrest the clergyman but to keep an eye on him.

Another Natchez minister who also refused to pray for a president, President Abraham Lincoln, was not as fortunate. During the Union occupation of Natchez, the bishop of St. Mary's Catholic Cathedral, William H. Elder, was arrested and briefly imprisoned at Vidalia, Louisiana, for violating a Union order requiring all clergymen to pray for the U.S. president. Elder was later released on the order of Secretary of War Edwin Stanton and, according to one historian, "amid the joyous ringing of bells and the acclamation of the citizens, the prelate returned triumphantly to his cathedral."

Johnny Reb, the common foot soldier of the Confederacy, like the Natchez conscripts, sometimes refused "to do duty" and often spoke of the Civil War as "a rich man's war and a poor man's fight." The common soldier's champion, James Zachariah George, claimed in the Mississippi Secession Convention that a war for Southern independence was to preserve the right of slavery, and that slave owners, therefore, ought to bear the burden of financing the war. He recommended a $1.25 tax per slave. Another delegate suggested a $2 tax on all slaves. Both proposals were defeated, however, and the Convention placed a small ad valorem tax on slaves, a tax established by slave owners who affixed the value of their slaves.

After the passage of the "20 Negro law" in September 1862, which provided military exemption to one white person on each plantation with 20 or more slaves, foot soldiers became even more disenchanted with the war, and desertion became a major problem for the Confederate military. In early 1865 a disheartened Robert E. Lee referred to desertion in the Confederate army as "an epidemic."

Although popular reaction to the "20 Negro law" was extremely negative, the law was not enacted for the benefit of rich planters or their sons. Only about 15 percent of the planters who were eligible for the exemption actually exercised their option. The law was prompted by widespread reports of slave unrest, like those reports coming out of Natchez in the fall of 1861. The chaos of war was a breeding ground for revolt, especially as advancing Union armies urged slaves to abandon their servitude. Whites who were left unprotected on widely scattered plantations wrote anxious letters to Confederate authorities, asking for some kind of protection.

Rumors of a slave revolt along Second Creek and Pine Ridge, communities just outside of Natchez, prompted the formation of a "vigilance" or "judicial" committee in September 1861 to interrogate slaves and to mete out punishment to those suspected of insurrection. Several slaves who were questioned by the vigilance committee freely admitted that they were planning a revolt. Although records are not clear on the number, several slaves were executed as a result of that investigation.

After Memphis fell on June 6, 1862, Adm. David Porter's gunboats descended the river toward Vicksburg, with Farragut, in the meantime, moving upstream from Natchez. Grant, however, was unable to reach Vicksburg overland from the northeast. He was bogged down in the swampy Delta flats which surrounded Vicksburg on the north and east.

When it became evident that Grant would be unable to reach Vicksburg by land, the combined naval forces of

Farragut and Porter shelled the Rebel fortress for several days in an unsuccessful effort to force its surrender. After that failure, Farragut returned to his base in New Orleans, and Porter remained anchored just north of Vicksburg. Grant, feeling checkmated, fretted through the winter of 1862, fearful that President Lincoln would grow impatient and relieve him of his command.

U.S. Adm. David D. Porter, about 1863

When the Union navy sealed off the Mississippi River at New Orleans and Memphis, several Confederate warships were stranded in a naval no man's land. Occasionally those ships encountered Union gunboats patrolling the river, and a battle ensued. On September 1, 1862, the *USS Essex*, which was in pursuit of the *CSS Webb*, docked at Natchez for fresh supplies. The small detachment sent ashore to get the supplies was attacked by about 200 armed citizens. One Union sailor was killed and six were wounded. The *Essex* retaliated by briefly bombarding Natchez Under-the-Hill. Later the *Essex* was fired on by the Silver Greys. Angered, the ship's commander ordered his gunners to shell the city for two

The USS Essex, *which fired on Natchez in 1862*

and one-half hours. Because of this attack, 7-year-old Rosalie Beekman died after being hit as she ran up Silver Street, away from her father's business establishment.

The editor of the Natchez *Courier,* while condemning the shelling as an "unmitigated outrage," reported that no one else was killed or wounded and that property damage in upper Natchez was very slight, though damage to lower Natchez was much more serious. Although there were other fatalities in Natchez during the Civil War, it is believed that Rosalie Beekman was the only person killed as a result of a military action.

By the spring of 1863 Grant had decided on a bold and dangerous assault against Vicksburg. He planned to march his army down the Louisiana side of the Mississippi River, then cross back into Mississippi and move against Vicksburg from the south, where the higher terrain would make a land assault of Vicksburg more practical. Grant's maneuver against Vicksburg began on March 29, when his troops started their long hike southward from Milliken's Bend, just north of Vicksburg.

The Federal occupation of Natchez in a scene in Natchez Under-the-Hill about 1863

Rosalie, 7, Sole *Essex* Victim

Rosalie Beekman, 7, was the sole victim of the bombardment of Natchez by the *USS Essex* in September 1862. The daughter of Fanny and Aaron Beekman, whose business was on Silver Street in Natchez Under-the-Hill, Rosalie was fleeing from the burning street with her family when she was hit by a shell and fell to the ground.

"I heard her fall," wrote Rosalie's sister, as quoted in Thomas Reber's *Proud Old Natchez*. "And (I) said to Papa, 'Rosalie has fallen down.' Papa called for her to get up.

"She said, 'I can't, Papa. I'm killed.' I remember his dreadful cries as he carried her in his arms, the blood streaming from her wound."

The little girl died the next day and was buried in the Natchez City Cemetery.

At Bruinsburg, a small river port south of Vicksburg, Grant met Porter's small fleet, which had run the guns of Vicksburg. Grant's large army and accoutrements of war were then ferried across the river back onto Mississippi soil. From Bruinsburg, Grant moved swiftly through Port Gibson, Raymond, Jackson, Edwards and finally to Vicksburg. After a 44-day siege, the impregnable fortress surrendered on July 4, 1863, only one day after the invincible general, Robert E. Lee, had been defeated at

Gettysburg. The news of those two defeats was a crushing blow to Confederate morale.

After the surrender of Vicksburg, the Federals controlled the Mississippi River, and President Lincoln announced that now the "The Father of Waters goes unvexed to the sea." Because Natchez, with its 200-foot high bluffs could vex the Great River if it were in Confederate hands, Grant ordered its occupation for the remainder of the war.

On the afternoon of July 13, 1863, Brig. Gen. Thomas E. G. Ransom and his forces began occupying the city, without resistance. He suspended civil government in Natchez and placed the town under martial law. The occupation of Natchez had been ordered partly because Union intelligence had learned that a large store of ammunition and other supplies had been assembled at Natchez for shipment to the eastern states of the Confederacy. Upon his arrival in Natchez Ransom found and captured a large cache of arms and ammunition, 5,000 head of cattle and an huge quantity of lumber.

Ransom also found that thousands of freedmen, as former slaves were called, had congregated at Natchez and were living in contraband barracks located along the riverfront north of the home Magnolia Vale. He asked his superiors, "What shall I do with them?" Since 1862 slaves had been considered military contraband and were subject to confiscation by the Union Army. Hundreds of thousands of the 4 million Southern slaves had been following the Union army since the beginning of the war. After the Emancipation Proclamation was issued on January 1, 1863, the number of freedmen fleeing their plantations increased even more. Like many other Southern towns, Natchez more than doubled in population in 1863.

In his report on the number of freedmen coming into Natchez, Ransom noted that there was one male for every six women and children. That imbalance was probably the result of the high enlistment in the Union Army among former slaves in the Natchez area. Before the

Federal forces taking possession of the Adams County Court-house in downtown Natchez in 1863

Emancipation Proclamation, the Union Army rarely enrolled black volunteers, even free blacks. Many Northerners doubted the slave's inclination or ability to fight for his freedom. The Navy, on the other hand, had a long tradition of enlisting blacks and was integrated from the start of the war. After emancipation, hundreds of black units were formed in the Union Army.

The South reacted to the enrollment of black troops with anger and outrage. President Jefferson Davis said it was the "most execrable measure in the history of man." The Confederate military command ordered its army to execute white officers of black units if any were captured.

African-American Civil War soldiers, about 1863

It is one of the great ironies of the Civil War that the Confederate Congress, after having condemned the enlistment of black troops in the Union Army, passed a law in 1865 authorizing the enlistment of blacks in the Southern army. According to the terms of the statute, blacks who enlisted in the Confederate Army would be freed after the war if the South won its independence. The war was over, however, before the law could be implemented.

In August 1863 Gen. Alonzo Thomas, adjutant general of the U. S. Army, came to Natchez to recruit black troops. Blacks responded with fervor to the opportunity to fight for their freedom. A total of 17,869 black Mississippians, many of them from the Natchez region, joined the Union Army during the Civil War. Mississippi provided about 10 percent of the 185,907 black Union military personnel.

During the Vicksburg campaign, in bloody hand-to-hand combat at Milliken's Bend in the summer of 1863, the First Mississippi Regiment of Colored Infantry, along with the Ninth and Eleventh Louisiana Colored Infantry,

A painting possibly depicting Congressional Medal of Honor winner John Wilson Brown of Natchez, who joined the U.S. Navy in 1862, on board the USS Hartford in 1864. Detail at left.

won the praise of Assistant Secretary of War Charles A. Dana. "The bravery of blacks at Milliken's Bend," he wrote, "completely revolutionized the sentiment of the army with regard to the employment of Negro troops."

Two young former Natchez slaves, Wilson Brown and Thomas Gates, boarded Adm. Farragut's flagship *Hartford* while it was anchored off Natchez in the spring of 1862 and joined the U. S. Navy. They were enlisted and sent to New Jersey for training. Brown was later assigned to the *Hartford*. For his acts of uncommon courage and by putting himself at great personal risk during the Battle of Mobile Bay on August 4, 1864, Wilson Brown won the praise of his skipper and the Congressional Medal of Honor. He was one of four black seaman to win the nation's highest military honor during the Civil War.

During the occupation of Natchez, several Federal officers commanded the Union garrison at various times. Two of them are studies in contrast, illustrating how very personal are the fortunes of war.

The first, Col. Thomas Kilby Smith, occupied the fabled Surget mansion, Clifton, during his command. In a letter to his wife, he boasted, "I have taken full possession of the house. Mr. and Mrs. (Francis) Surget are very subordinary personages. I fix the hours at which the gentleman and his wife shall eat and I...have all I fancy."

The Surgets' home was later demolished and a Federal fortification built on its site, reputedly because a Union officer felt slighted by not being invited to a party at the mansion. Years later Frank Surget said that if there had been a slight it was unintentional. He reportedly said, "I would have dined with the Devil himself if it would have saved Clifton."

The Surget home, Clifton, which was destroyed by Union forces, from Audubon's 1822 landscape of Natchez

Because of numerous complaints against Smith, he was relieved of his command by order of Gen. James B. McPherson. Brig. Gen. Walter Q. Gresham, a much more popular military leader, was appointed in his place. Gresham later served as secretary of state under President Grover Cleveland. According to a book by Mrs. Gresham, who spent two months in Natchez with her husband while living at the mansion Rosalie, the new

The mansion Rosalie, headquarters of the Union forces in Natchez in the 1860s, in a 1930 photograph

U.S. Brig. Gen. Walter Q. Gresham, commander of Natchez during the Civil War

commander was "zealous in protecting the people and their homes." Mrs. Gresham was very considerate of and courteous to Eliza Wilson, the owner of Rosalie, who during the war, occupied the upstairs quarters. The Greshams and Eliza Wilson became such good friends that after the war the Greshams returned to Natchez to visit her.

Grant also enjoyed a brief stay at Rosalie. Shortly after the fall of Vicksburg, while on his way to New Orleans to confer with Gen. N. P. Banks, Grant stopped at Natchez and spent a night at Rosalie, which was used as Union headquarters.

The federal garrison at Natchez numbered as many as 12,000 at one time but was greatly reduced when Grant and Sherman began their campaign in Tennessee and Georgia. The reduced force numbered approximately 1,200 white troops and 1,500 black troops. All were quartered at Fort McPherson, a fortification constructed on the Natchez bluff. The reduced Union garrison made Natchez a tempting target for Confederate forces in the area. In late July 1863 a Confederate cavalry unit attempted a raid at Natchez to obtain supplies and Negroes but was turned back by the Federals on the outskirts of town.

A much more serious Confederate attack on Natchez was made in December by Gen. Wirt Adams. With a sizable force estimated by the Federals to be somewhere between 2,500 and 4,000, Adams intended to retake Natchez. When McPherson learned that the town was threatened, he reinforced the garrison at Natchez. On December 8, Union and Confederate forces met a few miles from Natchez and engaged in a brief but hard fight. Turned back, Adams then moved downriver 21 miles and took a position at White Cliffs, where he could harass if not obstruct Union traffic on the river.

After he was prevented from retaking Natchez, Adams remained in the area for several months. He engaged in several skirmishes with Union troops and conducted forays against Unionists in the Natchez vicinity. A former resident of Natchez, Adams reported to his superior

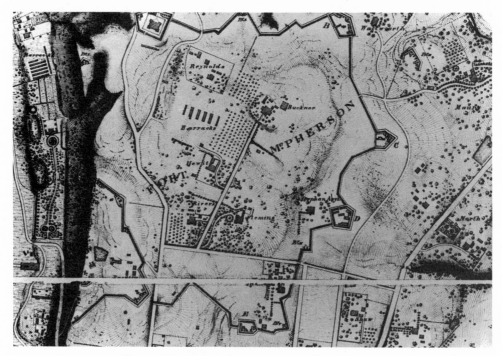

An 1864 map of Natchez showing Fort McPherson

Natchez Under-the-Hill, about 1864

officers that he was "burning all buildings, cotton, etc.,
upon the plantations of certain traitors about Natchez
and removing Negroes, stock, etc., for the use of the
government." The Natchez region not only tried to supply
the needs of its own residents, but it was also feeding
two armies. Planters suffered greatly from the hands of
both the Blue and the Gray.

For many Natchez planters the war was their ruin. As
the Federals approached New Orleans, Confederate
authorities burned $80 million worth of cotton. Some of
that cotton had been deposited by Natchez planters with
cotton commissioners in payment of their debts. Later,
as gunboats moved upriver toward Natchez, James
Surget, under the orders of the Confederate provost
marshal, burned 2,200 bales. His brother, Frank Surget,
wanted to take the oath of allegiance to the United States

after the Federal occupation but could not because the Confederate government held 500 bales of his cotton which he would have forfeited.

Almost all of the plantation stores of Alexander K. Farrar, a pre-war Unionist who was serving in the Confederate Army, were confiscated by the Federal army on September 23, 1864. Union troops hauled off 51 wagon loads of loose cotton and corn, 47 bales of cotton, and 143 head of cattle. Haller Nutt of the fabled octagonal mansion, Longwood, whose wealth had been based on land and slaves and cotton, said dejectedly, "I am ruined by this infernal secession."

By January 1865 Federal military authorities at Natchez began restoring some authority to civilian officials, and by late summer the difficult process of reconstruction was under way.

Approximately 300 of the Confederate soldiers from Natchez were killed in the war. Some of them are buried in the Natchez Cemetery along with three Confederate Generals and many other Civil War casualties. The National Cemetery at Natchez includes the remains of Wilson Brown, the former slave who won the Congressional Medal of Honor; 3,000 Civil War soldiers killed in nearby skirmishes; and 2,271 unknown Union soldiers.

Confederate notes, about 1862

Chapter 7
Reconstruction
and Rebuilding

Within months after the end of Civil War, a Republican newspaper was established in Natchez, appropriately called the *New South.* Both of the other Natchez papers accepted the Confederacy's defeat and the abolition of slavery, embraced the reality of a New South and advised their readers to do the same.

For Mississippi's 436,631 former slaves, emancipation was their jubilee day. They celebrated their new-found freedom with great commotion and great industry, and soon thereafter craved education. They stormed the citadels of learning where treasures of knowledge had been secreted from them during their years of bondage.

In 1864 Natchez had at least three schools for freedmen; in 1865 there were 11 such schools, with 20 teachers and more than 1,000 students of all ages. Two colleges were soon established to provide higher education for freedmen. One of them, the Natchez Seminary, was later moved to Jackson and became Jackson State University. The other, Natchez College, was established in 1885. Owned by the General Missionary Baptist State Convention of Mississippi, the liberal arts school has been a two-year college since 1952.

When an agent from the North-Western Baptist Missionary Convention arrived in Natchez in 1865, he found an eloquent ex-slave named Randall Pollard already preaching at the Rose Hill Baptist Church. Another Baptist church was built in Natchez on Pine Street at a cost of $2,800. In addition, Hiram Rhodes Revels was pastor of a large congregation at the newly established Zion Chapel African Methodist Episcopal Church. By the end of 1865 there were seven black churches in Adams County; five years later there were 18.

A session of the Freedmen's Bureau about 1865

Somewhat to the surprise of Southern whites who believed that former slaves would work only if forced to do so, freedmen embraced the free enterprise system with enthusiasm. Many invaded the ranks of black business, which had formerly been the exclusive domain of free men of color. Economic opportunities for former slaves in Natchez resulted in a large measure from the dramatic increase in the town's black population during and after the war. Blacks established concessions in the streets and on sidewalks where they sold such things as catfish and hushpuppies. Because there were so many such establishments, the city council restricted their activities to certain streets. Other former slaves became barbers, cobblers, storekeepers, seamstresses, painters, plasterers, draymen and craftsmen.

Some freedmen entered the professional ranks. There were at least four black attorneys practicing law in Natchez after the Civil War. Two of them were Lewis J. Winston, who also served a term as circuit clerk of Adams County, and Col. George Z. Bowles, who was described as a man of "elegant manner, immense dignity

Hiram Revels of Natchez, the first African-American to serve as U.S. senator

Zion Chapel AME Church on North Martin Luther King Jr. Street, established just after the Civil War

and high character." John Roy Lynch and his brother, William, became the most successful and most affluent black attorneys in post-war Natchez. Like many of his white peers had been doing for years, John R. Lynch sank his excess capital into land, becoming one of a small group of black landowners.

Among that select group were August and Sarah Mazique, who eventually acquired one of the plantations of their former owners. Before the war, the Maziques were the property of James Railey, a planter who owned Oakland and China Grove plantations. In 1870 August and Sarah Mazique purchased China Grove at a public auction. Their descendants subsequently acquired Oakland and approximately a dozen other plantations, including Bourbon, Montrose and Anchorage. The Mazique family's combined land holdings extended to several thousand acres.

For decades after the Civil War, the Maziques flourished as one of the most prosperous black planter families in the Old Natchez District. Their considerable influence in the Natchez black middle class was strengthened by marriage into the families of Dr. Albert Dumas

Alexander Mazique, son of August and Sarah Mazique, born in 1844, and his wife, Laura Craig Mazique, born in 1849, Natchez plantation owners after the Civil War

and Dr. Robert Harrison. The most famous of the Mazique clan was Dr. Edward Craig Mazique, a Washington, D. C. physician and civic leader. When he died in 1990, both President and Mrs. George Bush attended his funeral. First Lady Barbara Bush, who had known Mazique for several years, referred to him as "a leader, a role model and a thoughtful gentleman...a pioneer in so many ways."

Other freedmen and their descendants also prospered. The first African-American physician to practice in Natchez was probably Dr. J. B. Banks. Dr. Albert Dumas, another pioneering black physician, established a medical practice in 1899. Two of the earliest trained nurses in Natchez were Irby Robinson and Amanda Russell. Fraternal organizations and social clubs, which provided medical and burial expenses for their members, were very popular among blacks in Natchez and Adams County. Many of the organizations sponsored railroad excursions to Vicksburg and Jackson and steamboat rides on the Mississippi. In 1885 more than 20 black self-help and improvement societies existed in the Natchez area.

In the decade after the Civil War, Natchez achieved a level of political influence that it had not enjoyed since the 1830s. That new place of prominence was due primarily to the leadership of several people: John Roy Lynch, one of the first African-Americans to hold a public office in Mississippi; Hiram Revels, the first African-American to serve in the U. S. Senate, the first African-American to serve in either house of the U. S. Congress and the first president of Alcorn State University; Henry P. Jacobs, an influential member of the state legislature; and Natchez Mayor Robert H. Wood, the only African-American to serve as mayor of a Mississippi city during Reconstruction.

Lynch was appointed justice of the peace for Adams County in April 1869 and was elected to the state legislature the following year. His leadership skills won the esteem of his peers, who elected him Speaker of the State House of Representatives at the age of 24. In 1872 he was elected to the U. S. Congress and remained an influential member in state and national politics throughout the late 19th century. Lynch published three books and several articles in scholarly journals during his long and distinguished life. His autobiography, *Reminiscences of An Active Life: The Autobiography of John Roy Lynch,* describing his childhood in Natchez, is considered a classic in African-American literature.

Revels, while serving in the U. S. Senate, strongly and eloquently supported the measure to restore civil liberties to former Confederate officials and soldiers. Some say his support was instrumental in the passage of that legislation. In the early years of Reconstruction, Natchez was often cited by Mississippi Republicans as a showcase of bi-racial harmony, its African-American leadership winning the respect and cooperation of the Natchez-area white population. In his book, *The South: Its Indus-*

John Roy Lynch of Natchez, one of the first African-Americans to hold public office in Mississippi, in an 1869 portrait

trial, Financial, and Political Condition, published in 1886, Alexander K. McClure wrote that "Mississippi is exceptionable also in the reputable character of her most prominent colored leaders.... Hiram Revels and John Roy Lynch have maintained the manhood that should be the pride of every race."

The Natchez influence in Mississippi political affairs was also enhanced by its most famous resident carpetbagger, Gen. Adelbert Ames of Maine. Ames, who won the Congressional Medal of Honor at the first battle of Bull Run, was appointed provisional governor in 1868. After his military enlistment expired, he decided to remain in the state, eventually bringing his family to Mississippi. His wife was Blanche Butler Ames, daughter of the infamous Benjamin Butler, who commanded the Union occupation of New Orleans.

In search of a place to settle, Blanche Ames visited Natchez for four days in November 1870. She was very fond of the town and confided to her diary: "This place redeemed the South in my eyes.... It shows me that this state possesses more capabilities than I had given it credit for." She added that she was sorry that Gen. Ames was not yet ready to buy a home in Natchez.

Two years after her visit to Natchez, Ames did, in fact, purchase a house in Natchez. He wrote to his wife that he was also looking for a plantation to buy and hoped he could find a suitable one. In May 1873 Blanche Ames and the children joined Gen. Ames in Natchez. She wrote to her mother that the ladies of Natchez were courteous and respectful, but distant.

Blanche Butler Ames, wife of Gov. Adelbert Ames, in an 1878 portrait

Adelbert Ames of Natchez, elected governor of Mississippi in 1873

With the arrival of Adelbert Ames to Wilson Brown's home town, it is probable that Natchez was the only town in the South, and one of a few in the nation with a population under 10,000, that could boast of two Congressional Medal of Honor winners.

In the fall of 1873 Adelbert Ames was elected governor of Mississippi; his family moved with him to Jackson in early 1874. During the first two years of his administration, however, racial tension and partisan politics became so bitter that Ames was forced to resign in 1876 under threat of impeachment.

This threat was an indication that Mississippi's first attempt to establish a bi-racial society had failed, in part because white Mississippians were captive to a racial theory which held that blacks could not function in a state of freedom. The extremely high mortality rate among blacks in 1864 and 1865 led Gov. William Sharkey to predict that blacks would perish in a state of freedom within one generation. *The Natchez Democrat* agreed with the governor's assessment, writing in the fall of 1865 that "The child has already been born who will behold the last Negro in the state of Mississippi." The editor predicted that the race "will surely and speedily die out" without the white man's guardianship.

Some of the white residents of Natchez may have disagreed with the editor's prediction, but most of them would have agreed with his assertion that it might be acceptable for blacks to vote in Massachusetts but not in Mississippi. White Mississippians eventually rejected the idea of a bi-racial society, once more taking exclusive and total control of the state's political process.

While the political relationship between blacks and whites was being shaped by racial considerations, their economic relationship was being shaped by market conditions. As the historian Michael Wayne found in his study of post-Civil War Natchez, "The road to the New South plantation ran through the marketplace." He might also have added that it was a bumpy and winding road.

Looking west on Main Street, about 1900

Planters and freedmen entered their new and tenuous relationship with suspicion and skepticism. They haggled over contracts, which in the first few years after the war were vague and broad. As each party found the other interpreting the contract to his own advantage, each called for more specificity in the next year's agreement. Regardless of the individualized terms of the agreement, the very existence of a written contract between a planter and his field hands radically altered the social organization of the New South plantation.

Two successive crop failures in 1866 and 1867 had a lasting impact on Mississippi's system of agriculture. In 1866 Joseph Dunbar Shields, a Natchez lawyer, was pressed for payment on a plantation he had purchased. He told his creditor, "It would be a useless gratuity on my part to give you my note for it, for I have no more chance of redeeming it than [I have of] skating to heaven on a moonbeam."

Ironically, it was the worthlessness of the land that ultimately saved it for its owners. Land that was selling for $100 an acre in the 1850s sold for $50 or $55 an acre in the 1870s, if there were any takers. As a consequence of declining land values, many of the descendants of the great planters were able to hold on to their family properties, though most holdings were greatly reduced in size.

Land values and cotton prices continued in relentless decline, and, by 1890, sharecropping had replaced virtually all other labor arrangements. In the 1890 census 88.26 percent of all Adams County farmers were listed as tenants or sharecroppers. That year's crop of 1,209,000 bales brought about the same income that 306,000 bales had brought in 1866.

Although the old Natchez District lost its preeminence in the Cotton Kingdom, the town of Natchez became more prosperous after the war than it had been before. And it had not lost its pioneering spirit or its love for fun and frolic. In 1875 Natchez became the first town in Mississippi to hold a Mardi Gras celebration. Rex and his retainers arrived at the Natchez landing on a steamboat appropriately named "Royal Steamer." In the evening following a downtown parade, the Italian Society of Natchez held a gala Mardi Gras ball. Though the annual celebrating was discontinued in 1909, Natchez's Mardi Gras festivities were re-established in 1983.

Also after the war, the political and business leadership of Natchez realized the importance of a railroad that would link Natchez to other new lines extending into the interior of the state, especially to Jackson, which was fast becoming an important railroad junction. In 1870 a charter was secured for the Natchez-Jackson-Columbus Railroad Company. Columbus, the largest city in Northeast Mississippi, was linked to the Mobile and Ohio Railroad.

The effort to link Natchez with Jackson by rail had bipartisan support; both blacks and whites served on the company's board of directors. After overcoming many

*Newspaper story
about the Natchez
Mardi Gras in
1899*

A children's float in the Natchez Mardi Gras parade, about 1909

Celebrating the arrival of the first railroad engine, probably at Harriston, near Natchez, about 1900

financial and political obstacles, including the opposition of several other rival lines, the Natchez to Jackson line was completed in 1882. While city fathers were securing a railroad link with the interior of the state, they also continued to promote the town's river trade.

After the Civil War, several enterprising merchants arrived in Natchez to seek their fortunes, just as merchants had been doing from the town's earliest days. One of the most successful of the new merchants was Christian Schwartz, who in 1875 added a downtown mansion, Glen Auburn, to the town's parade of homes. Also among the new generation of shopkeepers were many Jewish families who brought a new energy and vitality to the town. The Jewish community in Natchez grew rapidly in the years following the war, constructing between 1870 and 1872 the state's first synagogue, Temple B'Nai Israel. This building burned in 1903 and was rebuilt in 1905.

In postwar Natchez as much as 90 percent of the mercantile trade was done on credit. Northern merchants who came to Natchez with a line of credit in New York, Philadelphia or Cincinnati had a substantial advantage over local merchants, whose credit had been suspended during the war or who were putting their capital in railroads and manufacturing. Unlike their

Glen Auburn on South Commerce Street, built in 1875 by Christian Schwartz

prewar predecessors, the new Natchez merchants did not sink their capital in land.

But due to the extremely short supply of Southern currency, new merchants did become a key element in the agricultural credit system of the New South. They advanced credit to planters and to sharecroppers throughout the growing season and settled with them at the harvest. Merchants usually insisted that sharecroppers grow only cotton, not even food crops. They preferred to furnish to farmers their supplies at a markup which averaged 60 percent. As the two Natchez banks gradually expanded, and as their deposits increased, they were able to ease the credit restraint, which was one of the most enduring legacies of the cotton market collapse.

The original Temple B'Nai Israel on South Commerce Street, built between 1870 and 1872, which burned in 1903.

During the last two decades of the 19th century, Natchez felt the ripples of the technological revolution that was changing the way Americans lived. Telephones were installed in Natchez in 1881, and electricity was brought to the city by Judge Thomas Reber in the early 1880s. An ice factory was founded in 1882, a new public transportation system was installed in 1886, running water and indoor plumbing became available in 1889 and a magnificent 5-story, 150-room hotel was opened in 1891. The new Natchez Hotel offered the most modern and up-to-date conveniences: elevators, electric lights, hot and cold running water, telephones and elegant dining facilities.

The city's public transportation facility at the time was a mule-driven trolley system planned and constructed by Reber. The original line extended from the ferry landing out up Silver Street to Main Street and St. Catherine Street, out to the intersection of Liberty Road. In 1905 the original trolleys were replaced by secondhand electric cars purchased from St. Louis. At its peak, the trolley system included five routes and served most of Natchez.

The Natchez Hotel, which opened in 1891 on the corner of Franklin and Pearl streets, in an 1895 photograph

An electric street car on Silver Street in Natchez Under-the-Hill, about 1909

One of Natchez's earliest automobiles, carrying Louise Unglaub, left, and an unidentified woman passenger and driver, about 1910

Paving Main Street, about 1908

WILLIAM HOWARD TAFT.

President Taft Visits Natchez

A highlight in Natchez right after the turn of the 20th century was the visit on October 29, 1909, of President William H. Taft to the city. On an official inspection tour of the Mississippi River, the president stopped at Natchez enroute to New Orleans. Natchez Mayor Benbrook extended a "most royal" welcome on the steamer Oleander, after which was a large parade of then new-fangled automobiles, which carried the dignitaries. Thousands crowded into Natchez for the parade and to hear the president's address on the Natchez Bluff. Because of the president's large size, a special chair for his use during the Bluff ceremony was loaned to him by the A.V. Davis family of Natchez.

When President William Taft paid a brief visit to Natchez on his way to New Orleans in 1909, he did not ride the trolley system. Instead, he was chauffeured in a new-fangled machine called the automobile, which Americans were just beginning to love. For many Natchez residents, especially for the country folks who came to town to see the president of the United States, it was their first glance at an automobile. But it would not be their last.

Natchez, like the rest of America, had its own love

affair with the automobile, and the year after the president's visit, the city began paving downtown streets in anticipation of the increased use of automobiles. The trolley system, eventually superseded by the "horseless carriage," was dismantled shortly before World War I.

The Natchez which President Taft visited in 1909 was a flourishing small Southern town eager to greet the opportunities of the 20th century, which was hailed even then as the century of progress and change. At the turn of this new century, Natchez had three banks, two cotton factories, two cotton seed mills, two lumber mills, an iron foundry, several brick kilns and cotton gins and a cotton compress capable of compressing 5,000 bales a day. There were also two daily and two weekly newspapers, a Jewish temple, a Catholic cathedral and perhaps Mississippi's first African-American Catholic church building (the Holy Family Church, whose cornerstone was laid in 1894). There were also Methodist, Baptist, Episcopal and Presbyterian churches and one of Mississippi's few public libraries.

In addition, there were about a dozen private schools and colleges, including Stanton College for white girls

Part of the Natchez Cotton Mills, about 1890

Choctaw on North Wall Street, home of Stanton College when this photograph was taken about 1900

The original building for Natchez College, established in 1885 on North Union Street, a building which burned in 1930

The Natchez Institute School on South Commerce Street, about 1900

Union School on the corner of Union and Monroe streets, built in 1871

and Natchez College, a coeducational institution for blacks. The antebellum Natchez Institute continued to provide public education at the elementary and secondary level for white children. Black children were provided similar instruction in a segregated public institution called the Union School.

The literary and cultural heritage of Old Natchez survived both the Civil War and the economic dislocation caused by the war. The town's love of sport also endured the long years of difficulty and depression. But the old Sport of Kings was gone, along with most of the other trappings of landed aristocracy and great wealth. By 1900 a more democratic and a much more popular sport had become the nation's favorite pastime: baseball. Natchez readily embraced America's new great game.

In 1902 Natchez joined with Greenville, Vicksburg and Baton Rouge, Louisiana, to form the original Cotton States League. The Natchez team, called the "Natchez Indians," in the league's first year won the pennant in what the Memphis *Commercial Appeal* described as "hot a championship race as pro baseball saw anywhere." After a see-saw season in which all four teams had a shot at the league title, Baton Rouge and Natchez were tied for the lead with a three-game series remaining to be played in Natchez.

BASE BALL.

Natchez outbatted Greenville yesterday but costly errors lost 'the game for them. Blackburn pitched and though the visitors potted eight hits with a total of fourteen bases; Natchez hit Becker for thirteen with a total of seventeen bases, besides getting two bases on balls.

News of the Natchez baseball team in The Natchez Daily Democrat, *about 1902*

Members of the Natchez Indians baseball team, about 1902

149

On September 8, 1902, more than 2,000 fans rode the trolley out to Old Concord Park to see Natchez take a one-game lead by beating Baton Rouge 11-1 in the series opener. The following day, an even larger crowd jammed Concord Park to see the Natchez Indians clench the Cotton States League's championship in an epic extra-inning game.

Also exciting during the early 20th century was the famed and fabled landing at Natchez Under-the-Hill. In the early summer of 1909 the most unusual and the most spectacular ship ever to call at Natchez anchored off its shore. On May 20, 1909, the *USS Mississippi*, a battleship, longer and wider than a football field, with a crew of more than 700, was moored off the Natchez landing. It was the biggest, heaviest and most awesome vessel ever to ply the interior reaches of the Father of Waters and the only first-class battleship ever to call at an inland port. It is said that every whistle and bell within miles of the waterfront heralded its approach to Natchez.

Commissioned on February 1, 1908, the *Mississippi* was brought to Natchez primarily through the efforts of a local businessman, Lemuel P. Conner. The *Mississippi* was scheduled to call at Horn Island on the Gulf Coast where Mississippi Gov. Edmund F. Noel was to present a silver tea service to the ship's captain on behalf of the people of the state.

Conner persuaded Natchez's city fathers to issue an invitation to the U. S. Navy to bring the *Mississippi* upriver from New Orleans to Natchez. After convincing the Navy that the Mississippi River could accommodate a battleship with a draw of 26.2 feet, naval authorities agreed to make the call at Natchez. The newly commis-sioned member of Theodore Roosevelt's Great White Fleet steamed up the mighty river at 15 knots, making the 297 miles from New Orleans to Natchez in a record time of 14 hours.

During the *Mississippi's* four-day stay at Natchez,

The USS Mississippi in 1909, when it visited Natchez

Officers of the USS Mississippi on the steps of the Prentiss Club on North Pearl Street, in 1909

more than 20,000 people visited onboard. Later, after World War I, the ship was sold by the United States to Greece, in accordance with the terms of an agreement between the United States and other world powers.

World War I, or—as those who lived through it called it, the Great War—brought many changes to Mississippi and to Natchez. One of the most significant of those changes was the new status of American women. Although Mississippi did not ratify the 19th Amendment, which gave women the right to vote in 1920, the city of Natchez and the county of Adams readily embraced the idea of a woman's right to vote and to hold office.

Josephine Virginia Fitts, first female superintendent of education in Adams County, in a 1905 photograph

In 1919, even before the amendment went into effect, Josephine Fitts of Natchez became Adams County's superintendent of education when she was appointed to fill the unexpired term of M. C. Montgomery. This first female superintendent, a graduate of Mississippi State College for Women (now Mississippi University for Women), was probably the first woman to hold a public office in the state of Mississippi. She was elected county superintendent in 1923 and remained in office until her retirement in the early 1950s.

Just as women had been influential in shaping Natchez's past, so, too, would they be instrumental in shaping its future as the city in the early 20th century entered uncertain years of depression, war and social revolution.

Chapter 8
The Renaissance of Old Natchez

During the 1920s, rural America in general and the Deep South in particular slipped into an economic downturn that by the 1930s had become the nation's deepest and longest economic depression. Since Mississippi was one of the states most severely affected by the Great Depression, it is ironic that in those extremely hard times, which were as bad as or worse than the conditions following the Civil War, there was a Renaissance of Old Natchez.

That rebirth began in the spring of 1931 when the Mississippi State Federation of Garden Clubs held its annual meeting in Natchez. To the enterprising women of the host club, the Natchez Garden Club, the state convention was a golden opportunity to publicize the history and heritage of Natchez, which they believed to be one of the town's most valuable resources. During the conference the Natchez Garden Club offered a special guided tour of several antebellum homes. Though tourists had been coming to Natchez for years, there had never been any organized or coordinated effort to promote tourism prior to that time.

That first tour in 1931 was so popular, and its potential in promoting the economic recovery of Natchez so evident, that the Natchez Garden Club planned a larger and better publicized tour in 1932. A nationwide publicity campaign, including speeches in Northern and Midwestern cities by Katherine Grafton Miller of Natchez, extolled the charm of Old Natchez and invited tourists from across the country to come to the first week-long Natchez Spring Pilgrimage in late March and early April 1932. Twenty-four houses were opened on that first Pilgrimage, which was such a success that with the

Three of the historic houses opened on the first Natchez Pilgrimage tour in 1932: top, The Elms, c. 1804; center, Gloucester, home of Territorial Gov. Winthrop Sargent; and Hope Farm, home of Spanish Gov. Carlos de Grand-Pre

Announcing
MRS. BALFOUR MILLER
(Originator of the Natchez Pilgrimage)

who gives an illustrated
talk on

"NATCHEZ, WHERE THE
OLD SOUTH STILL
LIVES"

Garden
Pilgrimage Week

March 28th through April 2nd
1932

❦

Natchez, Mississippi

"Where Shaded Highways and Ante-Bellum Homes
Greet New and Old Friends"

A brochure announcing the first Natchez Garden Pilgrimage Week, with house tours rotating daily from March 28 through April 2, 1932. The tours were so popular that an extra day of touring was added April 3. Houses opened that year were Homewood, Lansdowne, D'Evereux, Montaigne, Monmouth, Melrose, Linden, Arlington, Auburn, Hope Farm, Dunleith, Green Leaves, Airlie, Magnolia Vale, The Elms, Elms Court, Longwood, Gloucester, Elgin, Rosalie, Stanton Hall, King's Tavern, Richmond, The Briars, Ravenna and Clover Nook. Evening entertainment during the first Spring Pilgrimage included two cabaret-style dances, a concert of spiritual music called "Heaven Bound," a concert by The University of Mississippi Musical Club, a downtown parade with a Natchez history theme called "Under Many Flags" by Elizabeth Dunbar Murray, and two balls, one with kings and queens.

Katherine Grafton Miller, the "Originator of the Natchez Pilgrimage," on the cover of a brochure announcing her illustrated lecture, 'Natchez, Where the Old South Still Lives," which she presented in more than 75 cities nationwide in the 1930s and 1940s

exception of the war years of 1943, 1944 and 1945, the spring tour has been an annual event since 1932, growing to a month-long event soon after it began. An annual fall house tour was added in 1976, with year-round tours and a popular bed-and-breakfast program also added.

As part of the charm of Spring and Fall Pilgrimage, from the very beginning various evening entertainments have been presented, including the annual Confederate Pageant in the Spring which features live historical vignettes performed by hundreds of volunteers. Since the 1960s The Natchez Little Theatre has likewise entertained with a comedy called *Southern Exposure* which spoofs the Natchez Pilgrimage. Additional evening entertainments in the spring and fall include *The Mississippi Medicine Show, Southern Road to Freedom* and *The Drunkard, or, Down with Demon Drink!*

In 1932, while Katherine Miller, Edith Wyatt Moore and others were publicizing the charm of Old Natchez, a bizarre murder case involving two prominent families and their antebellum mansions captured national headlines and brought additional publicity to Natchez. This grisly tale of murder was serialized in several national magazines under the title "Murder with Southern Hospitality" and was later published in book form as *The Goat Castle Murder: A True Natchez Story That Shocked the World.*

Antebellum Glenwood, nicknamed "Goat Castle," in a 1932 photograph

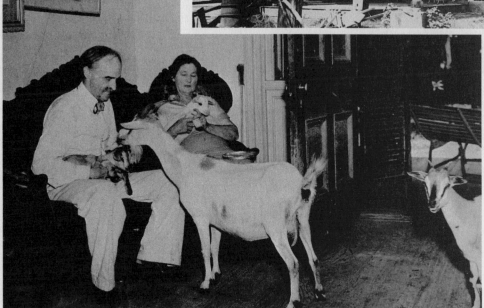

Dick Dana and Octavia Dockery at "Goat Castle" in 1932

Part of the fascination of the story was that goats roamed the first floor of a dilapidated Natchez mansion, Glenwood, "in undisturbed joy (while) chickens roosted on the foot of (a) great mahogany bed." In its former years, Glenwood was a stately home, but in the 1930s, because of its inhabitants, it was known as the "Goat Castle." Richard Dana, its owner, played an old piano for tips from tourists who came to see him and his house mate, both discredited aristocrats.

While he played the old piano, Octavia Dockery, Dana's court-appointed guardian, told stories of the couple's former wealth, reciting their lineage which reached into the Southern stratosphere, all the way up to Robert E. Lee and Jefferson Davis. In 1932 the pair was accused of murdering a neighbor, Jennie Merrill, a reclusive and wealthy spinster who lived at a nearby mansion, Glenburnie. Jennie Merrill had previously complained to local authorities about her neighbors' goats and chickens and had asked that something be done to keep them off her property. After a prolonged and sensational trial, which was covered extensively in the national and international press, the pitiful pair was acquitted.

The continued success of the Natchez Spring Pilgrimage, resulting from the Goat Castle murder and from all manner of other publicity, and the Pilgrimage's enormous revenue potential prompted in 1936 the formation of a second women's club, the Pilgrimage Garden Club, by 34 charter members who had formerly belonged to the Natchez Garden Club. In 1938 the Pilgrimage Club purchased the mansion Stanton Hall and made it the organization's headquarters. The Natchez Garden Club's headquarters during this time and for several decades thereafter was The House on Ellicott Hill, for many years called Connelly's Tavern. Current headquarters of the Natchez Garden Club is Magnolia Hall. Until 1942 the two clubs conducted separate house tours during the annual Spring Pilgrimage. However, since World War II, the clubs have jointly sponsored the event, which they

Some of the Natchez Pilgrimage leaders of 1937, seated from left, Ruth Audley Beltzhoover, Katherine Grafton Miller, Rebecca "Beck" Benoist, Clara S. Ballou and Lalie Adams; and standing from left, Alma Kellogg, Emma Marks, Mary Lambdin, Roane Byrnes and Edna Parker

National Historic Landmark Stanton Hall, built in the late 1850s, headquarters of the Pilgrimage Garden Club since 1938

The House on Ellicott Hill, formerly called Connelly's Tavern, on North Canal Street, a restoration project of the Natchez Garden Club, in before-and-after photographs in 1936 and 1940

continue to do today through Natchez Pilgrimage Tours, a year-round tourism business.

The popularity of the Spring Pilgrimage attracted a continuing flood of visitors to the city. Among the many with internationally known household names, who have visited Natchez are such governmental leaders as George Bush, Elizabeth Dole, Lady Bird Johnson, Manuel Lujan, Eleanor Roosevelt and Douglas MacArthur and such entertainment stars as Elizabeth Taylor, Frederick March, Helen Hayes, George Hamilton, Muhammed Ali and thousands more.

The popularity of Spring Pilgrimage also sparked a renewal of interest in the architectural heritage of Old Natchez. By the late 1930s and early 1940s, several mansions and other antebellum structures were being restored. After World War II a much more extensive restoration period occurred. In succeeding decades the Natchez Garden Club, the Pilgrimage Garden Club, the Auburn Garden Club, the City of Natchez, the Historic Natchez Foundation, the Natchez Historical Society, the Mississippi Department of Archives and History, the National Park Service and private enterprise have cooperated in Natchez in the preservation and restoration of one

THE NATCHEZ DEMOCRAT

Full Leased Wire Associated Press News Report

WORLD MARKETS

MRS. F. D. ROOSEVELT TAKES PART IN PILGRIMAGE

Neutrality Act Is Not Effective Says The President

A visit to Natchez in 1939 by First Lady Eleanor Roosevelt as reported in The Natchez Democrat

Actress Helen Hayes when she visited Natchez in 1989

Natchez Pilgrimage founder Katherine Grafton Miller dancing at Stanton Hall with 1952 Pilgrimage visitor Gen. Douglas MacArthur

Grace MacNeil, left, at her home, Elms Court, in 1970 with visiting actor Frederick March and his wife, Florence Eldridge March, center, and Anna Rose Metcalfe of The Parsonage

Black gold apparatus in a white gold field

An oil derrick, symbolic of the discovery of black gold in Adams County in 1945

of the largest aggregations of antebellum structures in the United States.

The Renaissance of Old Natchez was made possible partly by a bustling local economy which included farming, industry, timber and commerce, and in particular by the discovery of rich oil fields in Southwest Mississippi. In 1945 the first producing well was brought in at nearby Cranfield, the birthplace of the bestselling novelist Richard Wright. The well began producing in the same year that Wright's book, *Black Boy, A Record of Childhood and Youth*, was published. During the boom years of the 1950s, 1960s and 1970s, Natchez-area oil created thousands of jobs and quite a few fortunes. It became the No. 1 industry in Natchez, and the town prospered.

In addition to the discovery of oil, the Renaissance of Old Natchez was made possible by the addition of several other new industries, including Armstrong Tire and Rubber Company (later called Fidelity Tire Manufacturing Company), which was established in Natchez in 1939, International Paper and Manville Corporation (formerly

The International Paper Company plant at Natchez, about the time it was opened in 1949

called Johns-Manville), both of which were established in the mid 1900s.

At the same time, Natchez developed the Natchez-Adams County Airport and the Mississippi River Port and enjoyed the continuing local development of the Natchez Trace Parkway, a 450-mile national parkway begun in the 1930s which links Natchez and Nashville, Tennessee.

Other roads leading to Natchez were also developed, with four-lane highways linking the city north, south, east and west, culminating in 1989 with the completion of a new Mississippi River Bridge at Natchez to make that important link four-laned.

The Renaissance of Natchez owes a great deal to the continuing force of the city's quality educational institutions which offer everything from pre-school through college.

To assist the growing economic base of Natchez, in the 1970s a new bank, United Mississippi Bank, was established. It joined Deposit Guaranty National Bank (formerly City Bank and Trust Company), Britton & Koontz First National Bank, Magnolia Federal Bank and Natchez First Federal Savings Bank, all of which had been in business for decades.

All of Natchez's mid-20th-century business and educational activity caused the city to grow. But the primary strength was the rich earth. In the 19th century it had grown white gold to build the mansions; in the 20th century it issued black gold to refurbish them. And in the shadow of the new gray steel towers, the old white pillars flourished, fulfilling the prophecy that, at least in Natchez, "The South will rise again."

This fabled town, linked by lore and legend to an earlier, heroic age, during this more modern era began luring thousands of visitors every year to view the relics of a time, a place and a civilization that to many has "gone with the wind." Mint juleps served in the modern hotels and restaurants of Natchez may not be as transcendent as those served in the Mansion House Hotel in the 1850s, but the charm of these modern establishments is reminiscent of that lusty age, and their Old South connotations are irresistible.

One very important feature of the Renaissance of Old

Soon after the 1940 opening of the Mississippi River Bridge linking Natchez and Vidalia, Louisiana

LYNDA LEE, OUR OWN ★ MISS AMERICA ★

Natchez Beauty Is Chosen In Pageant Last Night

Natchez's Miss America

Lynda Lee Mead of Natchez, 20, called a "sloe-eyed Mississippi beauty" by the Associated Press, brought national attention to her home town by winning the Miss America title September 12, 1959, the second contestant in a row from Mississippi to do so. A junior at The University of Mississippi, Mead succeeded Mary Ann Mobley of Brandon, Mississippi, also an Ole Miss student. Mead's winning qualifications included green eyes, brown hair and skill as a dramatic actress. A parade and other festivities later welcomed her home to Natchez.

Natchez was the rescue of Natchez Under-the Hill from Old Man River and its resurrection as a place of fun and frolic. The history of Natchez Under-the Hill illustrates the triumph of place over time. This first riverside settlement to be called Natchez barely survived the advent of the railroad in the 1800s, and then only because it was the ferry landing which linked Natchez with Vidalia, Louisiana, and thence Texas and other points west of the Father of Waters.

In 1940 the wicked waterfront again faced extinction when the Natchez ferry was superseded by a glorious new bridge that spanned the mighty river. Over the next two decades the landing was all but abandoned, except for a few places like a night spot called the Blue Cat Club.

The Natchez ferry landing at Natchez Under-the-Hill about 1939, just before the Mississippi River Bridge at Natchez was completed

It was the area's infamous past, however, that eventually saved it and secured its future. Curious streams of tourists who came to see Natchez's stately mansions on top of the hill could not resist the pull of the landing's past, the power of its legends or the magic of its name: Natchez Under-the Hill.

By the mid-1970s Natchez Under-the-Hill was flourishing. Since then, spirited saloons, shops, restaurants, "Miss Floozie Contests" and late-night revelers have again enlivened Silver Street. The re-installation of riverboat gambling in the early 1990s will likely restore an additional aura of 18th- and 19th-century Natchez Under-the-Hill.

Flatboats and ferries of old might have faded away, but the 19th century's grand floating palaces made a stunning comeback in the 1970s, when Natchez Under-the-Hill again became a favorite port of call for magnificent steamboats. This new generation of steamboats, including two called *Mississippi Queen* and *Delta Queen.* rival in size, grandeur and elegance the legendary *Natchez* and

The **Delta Queen** *and the* **Mississippi Queen,** *the last of the paddle wheel steamboats which carry passengers on overnight cruises on the Mississippi River, docked at Natchez Under-the-Hill*

the *Robert E. Lee* while offering a leisured and unhurried journey back into America's past.

The Renaissance of Old Natchez was influenced also in part by a wave of nostalgia that rolled across the United States following World War II, especially after the Civil War Centennial of 1961-1965. Americans will forever be intrigued by their Civil War, which Mississippi historian Shelby Foote calls the defining event in this nation's history, and by the two civilizations--the North and the South--which waged that conflict. Perhaps Mississippi's Nobel Laureate, William Faulkner, was right when he said, "Nothing ever happens once, and it's over."

The 1970s were the most important years for historical preservation in Natchez since the 1930s. The Natchez Garden Club and the Pilgrimage Garden Club promoted restoration on a scale not attempted since their acquisition of "Connelly's Tavern" and Stanton Hall in the 1930s. During the early 1970s, the Pilgrimage Garden Club acquired the National Historic Landmark mansion Longwood as well as King's Tavern, a tavern on the old Natchez Trace which is believed to be the oldest extant building in Natchez. The Natchez Garden Club during this period secured Magnolia Hall, perhaps the last grand townhouse mansion built in America before the Civil War, as well as the House of William Johnson, the residence of the famous barber of Natchez. A third women's club, first called the Town and Country Garden Club and later called the Auburn Garden Club, accepted management responsibility for Auburn, Stephen

Magnolia Hall, 1858, the last great mansion built prior to the Civil War, headquarters of the Natchez Garden Club

Edgewood, 1859, an Italianate-style plantation ho

King's Tavern, 1790s, a tavern believed to have been a stop at the end of the Natchez Trace

Montaigne, 1855, surrounded by live oaks, azaleas and camellias

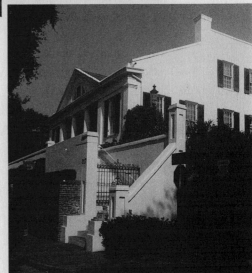

The Burn, 1836, noted for its semi-spiral staircase and lush gardens

Cherokee, c. 1794-1810, situated among colorful gardens

The Parsonage, 1852, overlooking the Mississippi River

Linden, c. 1800,
in a setting of
moss-draped cedars

Green Leaves, 1838, a downtown mansion
shaded by gigantic live oaks, in the same
family since 1849

Mount Repose, 1824,
a plantation house
that has never left
the family of the
builder

Duncan's 1812 mansion which his heirs donated to the city of Natchez in 1911.

In the 1970s the Natchez Garden Club and the Pilgrimage Garden Club also initiated two annual events that have proved culturally and economically beneficial to the community. The Pilgrimage Garden Club hosted its first Antiques Forum in 1974, and the Natchez Garden Club sponsored its first Antiques Show in 1976.

During that busy decade, the Historic Natchez Foundation was established in 1974. Its primary function, the preservation of Natchez neighborhoods and the downtown business district, is made possible in part by in-

Routhland, c. 1817, situated on a knoll in a park-like setting

Oakland, c. 1838, filled with Greek Revival wood work, high ceilings and fine architecture

come from the foundation's Historic Natchez Collection, which features copies of high-quality reproduction furniture and accessories found in Natchez houses. In 1979 the foundation employed its first full-time staff member, who immediately began obtaining National Register listings for the downtown and residential areas and otherwise promoting preservation.

Officials of the city of Natchez and Adams County also assumed a more prominent role in Natchez's preservation movement during the 1970s with the initiation of a county-wide survey of historic buildings. The findings of that survey provided information on which preservation controls were later based.

Natchez also benefited during this decade from state involvement in preservation and restoration. In cooperation with Natchez leaders interested in saving two important historic sites which were threatened, the state acquired them both through the Mississippi Department of Archives and History. These sites are the Grand Village of the Natchez Indians, which officially opened in 1976, and the campus of Historic Jefferson College at Washington, Mississippi, which opened in 1977.

With more than 600 antebellum mansions, houses, churches, commercial buildings and other structures in its immediate vicinity, Natchez has been aptly called a "Museum City of the Old South." Several Natchez city districts, numerous houses and other buildings are so significant that they are listed on the National Register of Historic Places; more than a dozen buildings also carry the prestigious title of National Historic Landmark. Because so much of Natchez is authentic Old South, since 1914 the city has attracted movie makers and television

One of many crews which have filmed movies and television shows in the Natchez area, here in Natchez Under-the-Hill in the 1980s

producers from as far away as Europe and Asia. Among the best-known feature films and television productions that include Natchez scenery are "Showboat," "Raintree County," "Horse Soldiers," "Huckleberry Finn," "The Autobiography of Miss Jane Pittman," "Freedom Road," "Beulah Land," "North and South" and the Disney production of Mississippi writer Willie Morris's childhood adventure, *Good Old Boy*.

Others attracted to Natchez include writers from around the world. Natchez has been a source or a setting for thousands of novels, histories, biographies, travelogues, short stories, essays, plays, poems and stories for newspapers, magazines, movies and television programs. These have been written by numerous outstanding authors, including Eudora Welty, James Michener, Walker Percy, Stark Young, Frank Yerby, James Street, Frank Slaughter, Cid Ricketts Sumner, Alice Walworth Graham, Michel Fabre, Robert V. Remini, Brooks Haxton and Evans Harrington. Natchez's storied history has served writers well; they have used it as a backdrop for everything from murder mysteries to tales of romance and intrigue to children's books.

Noted novelist Alice Walworth Graham, born in Natchez in 1905

Among the city's most prominent literary connections are Richard Wright, a great American black writer and author of *Native Son*, *Black Boy*, and *White Man, Listen!*; who was born near Natchez; Anne Moody, a human rights activist born in neighboring Wilkinson County and educated at Natchez College who is author of a classic account of childhood and youth, *Coming of Age in Mississippi*; and Ellen Douglas (Josephine Ayres Haxton), descendant of the first mayor of Natchez and an award-winning novelist. Among her major works are *A Family's Affairs*, *Black Cloud, White Cloud*, *Apostles of Light* (nominated for the National Book Award), *The Rock Cried Out* and *A Lifetime Burning*, selected for the 1982 Literature Award by the Mississippi Institute of Arts and Letters.

The heritage of leadership by Natchez statesmen is also continuing and flourishing in the late 20th century. Natchez has provided Mississippi a generation of leaders

Best-selling author Richard Wright, who was born near Natchez in 1908 and who spent part of his childhood in Natchez

Award-winning author Ellen Douglas, pen name of Josephine Ayres Haxton, born in Natchez in 1921

who are identified with the New South. Among that new generation are Bill Allain, who served the state first as attorney general and then as governor from 1984 to 1988; David C. Bramlette, U.S. District judge; Joseph S. Zuccaro, justice on the Mississippi Supreme Court; and Dr. Robert W. Harrison Jr., a native of Natchez who moved to Yazoo City, Mississippi, and became the first black Mississippian to serve on the Board of Trustees of State Institutions of Higher Learning. Perhaps unique in the history of Mississippi is that at one time in the early 1970s, two men from Natchez served concurrently as the top leaders in both houses of the Mississippi Legislature. Marion Smith was President Pro Tempore of the Mississippi Senate while John R. Junkin was Speaker of the House of Representatives. Each man also served as acting governor of Mississippi on numerous occasions.

Dr. Robert W. Harrison Jr., a Natchez native who was the first African-American to serve on the Board of Trustees of the Mississippi Institutions of Higher Learning, with his wife, Charlotte, a descendant of 19th-century Natchez Mayor Robert Wood.

Natchez native Bill Allain, governor of Mississippi from 1984-1988

Throughout the centuries, the story of Natchez has been a tale of two towns. With continuing popularity, the Spring and Fall Pilgrimages have emphasized Natchez's Old South heritage, while industrial expansion and a social revolution have shaped Natchez into a small, economically diversified town that is typical of the New South. Like most other towns in the New South, Natchez has experienced problems of economic fluctuations and challenges of racial readjustments.

Natchez was hard hit in the mid-1980s by a general downturn in the oil industry and a declining national economy. That economic slowdown highlighted the importance of tourism, which was by then one of the town's most important industries. Indeed, in the 1980s and 1990s many new tourism-related events were estab-lished in Natchez, many of which relate to the city's rich

The finale of the annual Natchez Spring Pilgrimage's Confederate Pageant, the presentation of the king and queen of Pilgrimage and their court; here in 1959, Queen Barbara Brandon and King George Armstrong

Fancy dress design, above, in an 1850s magazine, used as a pattern for Margaret Paxton Veller of Natchez, who wore the replica in the Natchez Spring Pilgrimage's Confederate Pageant in the 1940s and 1950s

history and culture. These events include Mardi Gras each winter, resurrected from similar carnivals held in Natchez in the late 1880s and early 1900s; the Natchez Opera Festival, reviving an age when steamboats regularly brought top musicians to the city; the Natchez Literary Celebration, which focuses on Natchez's history, literature and culture, an event begun by Copiah-Lincoln Community College in 1990 and later co-sponsored by the college and the Natchez National Historical Park; the Great Mississippi River Balloon Race, reminiscent of ballooning in Natchez in the 19th century; the Mississippi Heritage Festival, recalling music, food and fun of days long ago; the Natchez Bicycle Classic, an updated, competitive version of the historic pastime of bicycling; and Victorian Christmas in Natchez, a month-long celebration of Christmas each December, with tours of gaily decorated historic houses, musical events and special meals and entertainments, all much like those in the 19th century.

It is ironic that in the 1980s, with the solid growth of tourism in Natchez, the city's past also became its future, a fact which complicated race relations.

During the Civil Rights Movement of the 1960s and 1970s, Natchez had many problems, but the city did not experience the degree of racial bitterness and violence that divided many other Southern towns. Beginning in the early days of the Pilgrimage, blacks had joined whites in presenting Natchez to tourists. Blacks were featured in one of the Pilgrimage's most loved Confederate Pageant tableaux, and in addition, a popular musical program called "Heaven Bound," which regularly attracted large audiences, was presented by blacks.

However, as the movement for racial justice and equal opportunity intensified in the 1960s, many blacks became ambivalent about celebrating the past, a time when King Cotton and slave labor were the basis of Southern wealth. They declined to perform the traditional black roles in the Confederate Pageant, and "Heaven Bound" was discontinued.

Some blacks at this time contended that they did not materially benefit from tourism; they urged the city to redirect its effort toward securing new jobs related to other businesses. Other black leaders recognized the importance of tourism and some, like Phillip West, the first black president of the Adams County Board of Supervisors, argued that the Old South could coexist with the New South "as long as," he said, "people recognize today as reality and what today's world calls for."

In the 1960s, '70s and '80s, while the public school system, governmental agencies and all other public facilities were being totally integrated, Natchez's black and white leaders sought ways to reconcile the past with the present. An important step in that direction was taken in the late 1980s when a musical tribute celebrating the African-American experience in Natchez became a part of the annual Pilgrimage.

Soon thereafter the history of blacks in Natchez was given special emphasis with the development of a bro-

HEAVEN BOUND LAST NIGHT WAS VERY ENJOYABLE

Splendid Presentation Of Negro Spiritual Witnessed By Large Number—All High In Praise

Heaven Bound, negro spiritual which has been presented in connection with the Pilgrimage of the Natchez Garden Club for five years, was a feature evening entertainment presented yesterday.

The spiritual is presented by a cast of about one hundred untrained, but exceptionally good negro voices. They rendered solos and chorus numbers.

A 1937 Natchez Democrat report of the success of "Heaven Bound," an evening entertainment which featured spirituals

Fair Oaks, 1822, a Federal-style plantation home in the same family since 1856

Mistletoe, 1811, a plantation home still in the family of the builder, John Bisland

Hawthorne, c. 1814, a Federal-style home with outstanding interior architectural features

Elgin, c. 1792-1855, a plantation home surrounded by 25 acres of gardens

Texada, 1792, once a tavern, hotel and Territorial legislative hall and now a downtown home

chure, a tour, a slide program and a museum devoted to various aspects of black culture, all available for tourist groups and the general public. Natchez Convention and Visitor Bureau employed a minority tourism director. The past, rather than dividing Natchezians, was becoming a bridge between them.

Perhaps the best measure of the progress Natchez has made in the effort to celebrate the diversity of its heritage is found in a statement made by Vernon E. Jordan Jr., former president of the National Urban League, when he contrasted two of his visits to Natchez. In 1962 Jordan visited Natchez to demonstrate against segregation and racial injustice at the invitation of Mississippi Civil Rights leader Medgar Evers, who was later murdered by a sniper's bullet. Jordan and Evers stayed in the home of a Natchez black leader because public accommodations were then segregated.

When Jordan visited Natchez nearly 30 years later, in 1990, to address the annual Southern Governors Conference, he was invited by the governor of Mississippi to stay at Monmouth, a mansion which was formerly the home of John A. Quitman, one of Mississippi's antebellum governors. Jordan contrasted his first visit to Natchez with the second by observing, "Today Natchez is open, warm, hospitable and desegregated.... Medgar's blood was not shed in vain."

The year after Jordan offered that assessment of Natchez, an important new dimension was added to the celebration of Natchez's heritage. In 1991 the home of William Johnson, Mississippi's most famous and most successful free black, was officially dedicated and conveyed to the National Park Service as a permanent site in the Natchez National Historical Park. This park, which is the southern origin of the Natchez Trace Parkway, also includes the magnificent mansion, Melrose, dedicated to the Park Service in 1990.

The Natchez National Historical Park, which will eventually include other Natchez historic sites, will commemorate and secure for future generations the history

Noted Natchez band leader Bud Scott, born about 1858, whose music delighted three U.S. presidents and countless others until his death in 1938

The 1841 home of William Johnson, a free man of color known as "the Barber of Natchez," on State Street prior to its restoration.

The 1845 mansion Melrose on Melrose Avenue, acquired in 1990 by the National Park Service as the first portion of the Natchez National Historical Park

and charm of antebellum Natchez, the oldest settlement on America's Great River. The heritage of the Natchez Indians and the legacies of three nations, along with the traditions of rugged frontiersmen, free men of color and great planters, shaped a social order in Old Natchez that is unique in American history.

The grace and grandeur of that society continue to linger in America's historical memory, as thousands of visitors each year are lured to Natchez. Here people can easily clasp hands with history as they stroll the streets, stand along the banks of the Great River and absorb the city's sights, sounds, smells and scenery.

Natchez, a unique gem of a place, gleams with many facets, all of which reflect a multi-hued history and all of which prove the city is truly one of America's most precious jewels.

Appendix A

Modern-Day Natchez at a Glance

Altitude, location, climate and population

Natchez, 195 feet above sea level, is the western-most city in Mississippi and the county seat of Adams County. The city's average January temperature is 49 degrees, the average July temperature is 82 degrees and the total annual rainfall is 57 inches. The only incorporated city in Adams County, Natchez in the 1990 census had 19,460 residents, while Adams County had 35,356.

Educational institutions

The Natchez Public School System operates four elementary schools, one middle school and one high school for the county. Other schools offering pre-school through 12th grade are two parochial schools, Cathedral (Catholic) School and Trinity Episcopal Day School, and one private school, Adams County Christian School. Other schools offering elementary and/or special education are Holy Family Catholic School, Maranatha School and Pleasant Acre Day School.

Higher education is offered by three institutions: (1) Copiah-Lincoln Community College, a public two-year commuter college offering academic, vocational-technical and other programs, including the international Elderhostel program and the internationally known Natchez Literary Celebration; (2) Natchez College, a two-year liberal arts school owned by the General Missionary Baptist State Convention of Mississippi; and (3) Alcorn State University School of Nursing, which offers a variety of upper-level courses in addition to nursing classes.

Government

The City of Natchez is governed by a mayor and six aldermen. Adams County is governed by a five-person board of supervisors, which elects its own president.

Health and medical facilities

Adams County is served by two hospitals: Jefferson Davis Memorial Hospital and Humana Hospital-Natchez. The county is also served by three nursing homes.

Appendix B

City of Natchez Population, 1810-1990

	SLAVES	WHITES	FREE BLACKS	TOTAL
1810	459	1,021	31	1,511
1820	654	1,468	82	2,204
1830	1,187	1,527	75	2,789
1840	1,599	2,994	207	4,800
1850	1,511	2,710	213	4,434
1860	2,132	4,272	208	6,612

	BLACKS	WHITES	OTHERS	TOTAL
1870	5,329	3,728		9,057
1880	3,637	3,421		7,058
1890	5,241	4,858	2	10,101
1900	7,090	5,11	4	12,210
1910	6,700	5,087	4	11,791
1920	6,801	5,80	4	12,608
1930	7,159	6,258	5	13,422
1940	8,001	7,287	8	15,296
1950	9,958*	12,782		22,740
1960	12,343	11,437	11	23,791
1970	9,959	9,733	12	19,704
1980	11,447*	10,514		21,961
1990	9,796	9,596		19,460 **

*Includes all non-whites
**Other races not included in this total
SOURCE: U.S. Census 1810-1990

For Further Reading

Abernathy, Thomas P. *The Burr Conspiracy.* New York, 1954.

Alford, Terry. *Prince Among Slaves, The True Story of an African Prince Sold into Slavery in the American South.* New York, 1977.

Ames, Blanche. *Adelbert Ames 1835-1933.* New York, 1964.

Ames, Blanche B. *Chronicles from the Nineteenth Century.* 2 vols Clinton, Mass., 1957.

Baldwin, Joseph G. *The Flush Times of Alabama and Mississippi, A Series of Sketches.* New York, 1853.

Barney, William. *The Secession Impulse: Alabama and Mississippi.* Princeton, 1974.

Bearrs, Edwin C. *Decision in Mississippi.* Little Rock, Ark., 1962.

Bearrs, Edwin C. *Rebel Victory at Vicksburg.* Vicksburg, Miss., 1963.

Bettersworth, John K. *Confederate Mississippi, The People and Policies of a Cotton State in Wartime.* Baton Rouge, La., 1943.

Blain, Walter, and Franklin J. Meine. *Half Horse Half Alligator: The Growth of the Mike Fink Legend.* Chicago, 1956.

Blain, William T. *Education in the Old Southwest: A History of Jefferson College.* Washington, Miss., 1976.

Blassingame, John W. *The Slave Community: Plantation Life in the Antebellum South.* New York, 1979.

Brown, Alexander D. *Grierson's Raid.* Urbana, Ill., 1954.

Brown, Dale C., Mary B. Eidt, Joan W. Gandy and Carolyn Vance Smith. *The Complete Guide to Natchez.* Natchez, Miss., 1977.

Brown, Dale Campbell, Mary B. Eidt, Joan W. Gandy and Carolyn V. Smith. *Stanton Hall: Natchez.* Natchez, Miss., 1980.

Burt, Jessie, and Robert Ferguson. *Indians of the Southeast Then and Now.* Nashville, Tenn., 1973.

Butler, Pierce. *The Unhurried Years: Memories of the Old Natchez Region.* Baton Rouge, La., 1948.

Callon, Sim C., and Carolyn Vance Smith. *The Goat Castle Murder: A True Natchez Story That Shocked the World.* Natchez, Miss., 1985.

Carter, Hodding. *The Lower Mississippi.* New York, 1942.

Claiborne, J. F. H. *Mississippi as a Province, Territory, and State with Biographical Notices of Eminent Citizens.* Jackson, Miss., 1880.

Clark, Thomas D., and John D. W. Guice. *Frontiers in Conflict, The Old Southwest, 1795-1830.* Albuquerque, N. M., 1989

Coates, Robert. *The Outlaw Years: The History of Land Pirates of the Natchez Trace.* New York, 1930.

Collier, Louise. *Pilgrimage: A Tale of Old Natchez.* Memphis, Tenn., 1982.

Cooper, J. Wesley. *Natchez, a Treasure of Antebellum Homes.* Philadelphia, 1957.

Crutchfield, J. A. *The Natchez Trace: A Pictorial History.* Nashville, Tenn., 1985.

Cushman, Horatio B. *History of the Choctaw, Chickasaw, and Natchez Indians.* New York, 1972. Reprint, 1899 Edition.

Daniels, Jonathan. *The Devil's Backbone: The Story of the Natchez Trace.* New York, 1962.

Davis, Edwin, and William R. Hogan. *The Barber of Natchez.* Baton Rouge, La., 1954.

Davis, Ronald. *Good and Faithful Labor: From Slavery to Sharecropping in the Natchez District, 1860-1890.* Westport, Conn., 1982.

Davis, Varina Howell. *Jefferson Davis: Ex-President of the Confederate States of America, A Memoir by His Wife.* 2 vols. New York, 1890.

DeRosier, Arthur H. Jr. "William Dunbar: A Product of the Eighteenth Century Scottish Renaissance." *Journal of Mississippi History* 28 (1966): 185-227.

Dickey, Dallas C. *Seargent S. Prentiss, Whig Orator of the Old South.* Baton Rouge, La., 1945.

Dow, Lorenzo. *Cosmopolite Interrogated, or, A Dialogue Between the Curious and Singular.* New York, 1813.

Eaton, Clement. *Jefferson Davis.* New York, 1977.

Elder, William. *Civil War Diary of Bishop William Henry Elder.* Natchez, 1960.

Fabre, Michel. *The World of Richard Wright.* Jackson, Miss., 1985.

Foote, Shelby. *The Civil War: A Narrative.* 3 vols. New York, 1986.

Frank, Joseph III. "In Defense of Hutchins' Indian." In *Anthology of Mississippi Archeology, 1966-1979.* Ed. Patricia K. Galloway, 83-85. Jackson, Miss., 1985.

Galloway, Charles Betts. "Aaron Burr in Mississippi." *Publications of the Mississippi Historical Society* 10 (1909): 237-247.

Galloway, Patricia K., ed. *LaSalle and His Legacy: Frenchmen and Indians in the Lower Mississippi Valley.* Jackson, Miss., 1983.

Galloway, Patricia K., ed. *LaSalle, the Mississippi, and the Gulf.* College Station, Texas, 1987.

Galloway, Patricia K., ed. *Mississippi Provincial Archives: French Dominion.* 2 vols. Baton Rouge, La., 1984.

Galloway, Patricia K. *The Southeastern Ceremonial Complex: Artifacts and Analysis.* Lincoln, Neb., 1989.

Gandy, Joan W., and Thomas H. Gandy. *Norman's Natchez: An Early Photographer and His Town.* Jackson, Miss., 1978.

Garner, James. *Reconstruction in Mississippi.* New York, 1901.

Gleason, David King, Mary W. Miller and Ronald W. Miller. *Great Houses of Natchez.* Jackson, Miss., 1988.

Graham, Alice Walworth. *Natchez Woman.* New York, 1950.

Green, Robert. *Black Defenders of America 1775-1973.* Chicago, 1974.

Gresham, Matilda. *Life of Walter Quintin Gresham 1832-1895.* 2 vols. Chicago, 1919.

Harris, William C. *The Day of the Carpetbagger.* Baton Rouge, La., 1979.

Haynes, Robert V. *The Natchez District and the American Revolution.* Jackson, Miss., 1976.

Hogan, William R., and Edwin A. Davis, eds. *William Johnson's Natchez: The Ante-Bellum Diary of a Free Negro.* Baton Rouge, La., 1951.

Holmes, Jack D. L. *Gayoso, the Life of a Spanish Governor in the Mississippi Valley, 1789-1799.* Baton Rouge, La., 1965.

Hudson, Charles. *The Southeastern Indians.* Knoxville, Tenn., 1976.

Ingraham, Joseph Holt. *The South-West, by a Yankee.* New York, 1835.

James, D. Clayton. *Antebellum Natchez.* Baton Rouge, La., 1968.

Johnson, Cecil. *British West Florida, 1763-1783.* New Haven, Conn., 1943.

Jordan, Winthrop D. *Tumult and Silence at Second Creek: An Historical Inquiry into a Slave Conspiracy, Adams County, Mississippi, 1861.* Baton Rouge, La., 1992.

Kane, Harnett T. *Natchez on the Mississippi.* New York, 1947.

Keating, Bern. *Natchez and the Trace.* Jackson, Miss., 1982.

La Page du Pratz. *A History of Louisiana.* New Orleans, 1947.

Lloyd, James B., ed. *Lives of Mississippi Authors, 1817-1967.* Jackson, Miss., 1981.

Lynch, John Roy. *The Facts of Reconstruction.* Ed., with Introduction, William C. Harris. New York, 1970.

Lynch, John Roy. *Reminiscences of an Active Life: The Autobiography of John Roy Lynch.* Ed., with Introduction, John Hope Franklin. Chicago, 1970.

May, Robert. *John A. Quitman, Old South Crusader.* Baton Rouge, La., 1985.

McAdams, Ina May. *The Building of Longwood.* Austin, Texas, 1972.

McLemore, Richard A., ed. *A History of Mississippi.* 2 vols. Jackson, Miss., 1973.

McMillen, Neil R. *Dark Journey: Black Mississippians in the Age of Jim Crow.* Urbana, Ill., 1989.

McPherson, James E. *The Battle Cry of Freedom, The Civil War Era.* New York, 1988.

McRaney, Joan Warren, and Carolyn Vance Smith, eds. *Silhouettes of Settlers.* Natchez, Miss., 1974.

McWilliams, Richebourg G., ed. *Fleur de Lys and Calumet: Being the Penicaut Narrative of French Adventure in Louisiana.* Baton Rouge, La., 1963.

Michener, James. *Texas.* New York, 1985.

Miles, Edwin. *Jacksonian Democracy in Mississippi.* New York, 1961.

Miller, Katherine Grafton. *Natchez Is a Fairy Story.* Natchez, Miss., 1974.

Miller, Mary W., and Ronald W. Miller. *Natchez, A Walking Guide to the Old Town.* Natchez, Miss., 1985.

Moore, Edith Wyatt. *Natchez Under-the-Hill.* Natchez, Miss., 1958.

Moore, John Hebron. *Agriculture in Antebellum Mississippi.* New York, 1958.

Moore, John Hebron. *The Emergence of the Cotton Kingdom in the Old Southwest, Mississippi 1770-1860.* Baton Rouge, La., 1988.

Oliver, Nola Nance. *Natchez, Symbol of the Old South.* New York, 1940.

Oliver, Nola Nance. *This Too Is Natchez.* New York, 1953.

Percy, Walker. *The Moviegoer.* London, 1963.

Pishell, Robert. *Natchez, Museum City of the Old South.* Tulsa, Okla., 1959.

Polk, Noel, ed. *Natchez before 1830.* Jackson, Miss., 1989.

Power, Major Steve. *The Memento, Old and New Natchez 1700 to 1897.* Natchez, Miss., 1897.

Rainwater, Percy L. *Mississippi, The Storm Center of Secession.* Baton Rouge, La., 1938.

Reber, Thomas. *In Old Natchez.* Natchez, Miss., 1909.

Remini, Robert V. *The Life of Andrew Jackson.* New York, 1988.

Ross, Ishbel. *First Lady of the South, The Life of Mrs. Jefferson Davis.* New York, 1958.

Rothstein, Morton. "The Natchez Nabobs: Kinship and Friendship in an Economic Elite." In *Toward a New View of America: Essays in Honor of Arthur C. Cole.* New York, 1977.

Rothstein, Morton. "The Remotest Corner': Natchez on the American Frontier." In *Natchez Before 1830,* ed. Noel Polk, Jackson, Miss., 1989.

Rowland, Dunbar. *Mississippi Comprising Sketches . . . Arranged in Cyclopedic Form.* 3 vols. Jackson, Miss., 1935.

Rowland, Eron. *Life, Letters, and Papers of William Dunbar of Elgin, Morayshire, Scotland, and Natchez, Mississippi: Pioneer Scientist of the Southern United States.* Jackson, Miss., 1930.

Sansing, David G. *Making Haste Slowly, the Troubled History of Higher Education in Mississippi.* Jackson, Miss., 1990.

Scarborough, William K. "Heartland of the Cotton Kingdom." In *A History of Mississippi,* ed. Richard A. McLemore, 310-352, Jackson, Miss., 1973.

Scarborough, William K. *The Overseer: Plantation Management in the Old South.* Baton Rouge, La., 1966.

Sewell, George, and Margaret L. Dwight. *Mississippi Black History Makers.* Jackson, Miss., 1984.

Shenton, James P. *Robert J. Walker: A Politician from Jackson to Lincoln.* New York, 1961.

Shields, Joseph D. *Natchez: Its Early History.* Louisville, Ky., 1930.

Slaughter, Frank. *Flight from Natchez.* New York, 1956.

Smith, Carolyn Vance. *Secrets of Natchez from a Journalist's Notebook.* Natchez, Miss., 1984.

Smith, Reid, and John Owens. *The Majesty of Natchez.* Montgomery, Ala., 1969.

Stratton, Joseph B. *Diary.* Unpublished, mid 19th century.

Street, James. *By Valor and Arms.* New York, 1944.

Sumner, Cid Ricketts. *Tammy Out of Time, a Novel.* Chicago, 1948.

Swanton, John. *Indians of the Lower Mississippi Valley and Adjacent Coast of the Gulf of Mexico.* Washington, D.C., 1911.

Sydnor, Charles. *A Gentleman of the Old Natchez Region: Benjamin L.C. Wailes.* Durham, N.C., 1938.

Sydnor, Charles. *Slavery in Mississippi.* New York, 1933.

Taylor, William B. *King Cotton and Old Glory.* Hattiesburg, Miss., 1977.

Van Court, Catherine. *In Old Natchez.* New York, 1937.

Wayne, Michael. *Reshaping of Plantation Society: The Natchez District, 1860-1880.* Baton Rouge, La., 1983.

Wellman, Manley Wade. *The Fastest on the River: The Great Race Between the Natchez and the Robert E. Lee.* New York, 1957.

Welty, Eudora. *The Robber Bridegroom.* New York, 1942.

Wharton, Vernon L. *The Negro in Mississippi, 1865-1890.* Chapel Hill, N. C., 1947.

Whitwell, William L. *The Heritage of Longwood.* Jackson, Miss., 1975.

Wood, Lucianne, and Sarah Webster Harrison. *Rosalie, A Mansion of Natchez.* Natchez, Miss., 1978.

Young, Harold, and Patti Carr Black. *The Natchez Trace.* Jackson, Miss., 1989.

Young, Stark. *So Red the Rose.* New York, 1934.

Acknowledgments

This book was inspired by an original illustrated lecture presented by David G. Sansing and Sim C. Callon at the second annual Natchez Literary Celebration in Natchez, Mississippi, May 29-June 1, 1991. This conference, co-sponsored by Copiah-Lincoln Community College and the Natchez National Historical Park, was co-chaired by Carolyn Vance Smith and Becky Junkin Nevill of Copiah-Lincoln and Stuart Johnson of the National Park. The lecture program of the conference was financially assisted by the National Endowment for the Humanities through the Mississippi Humanities Council.

The authors wish to acknowledge the assistance of many people who helped make this book possible.

Special thanks go to Marion Kelly Ferry, formerly of Natchez, and her family for making available the 1822 painting of Natchez by the naturalist/artist John James Audubon, which is used on the cover of this book. Special thanks also go to Mary Warren Miller of the Mississippi Department of Archives and History in Natchez, who served as historical consultant for the book. Thanks also go to James F. Barnett Jr., Elizabeth MacNeil Boggess, James Browning, Thomas H. Gandy and Marion Smith, all of Natchez, who read parts of this book in manuscript form and made many helpful suggestions. Others to whom the authors are grateful are William M. Smith Jr. of Natchez, who rendered the maps appearing in the book; Ronald W. Miller and his staff at the Historic Natchez Foundation; and Elbert Hilliard and staff members, Mississippi Department of Archives and History, Jackson, Mississippi. Colleagues who assisted at The University of Mississippi are Dr. Thomas Verich, Naomi Leavell and Sharon Sarthou of the Special Collections Division, John Davis Williams Library; Ginger Delk, administrative secretary, and Vickie Woodall, secretarial staff member, Department of History; and Max Williams, Director of the Center for Population Studies. Thanks also go for the support of Copiah-Lincoln Community College administrators Dr. Billy B. Thames, Dr. Howell C. Garner and Dean Travis Thornton, secretary Pat Cater and librarian Joan McLemore. Others assisting were staff members of both the Copiah-Lincoln Community College Library in Natchez and the Judge George W. Armstrong Library in Natchez.

Thanks also go to *The Natchez Democrat*, a daily newspaper, and its publishers, editors and managing editors in the 1980s, including Dolph Tillotson, John Mathew, Jim Morgan, Warren Johnston,

Harrison Cochran, Jennifer Allen and Dave Balcom. Much of the research utilized in this book was done for *Democrat* stories by Carolyn Vance Smith while she worked with these professionals.

Others to whom the authors are grateful are the following, for assistance with the photographs and other illustrations which appear in this book: Kate Don Adams, Judge George W. Armstrong Library, Auburn Garden Club, Caroline Benoist, Peggy Benson, Rawdon Blankenstein, Sim C. Callon Jr., Alma Carpenter, Donald Covington, Delta Queen Steamboat Co., the late Joseph F. Dixon, Marion Kelly Ferry, Alice Walworth Graham, the late Martha Guthrie, Robert and Julia Harrison, Kenneth M. Hathaway, Emily Haxton, Josephine Ayres Haxton (Ellen Douglas), Carl Hicks, Historic Natchez Foundation, Edna Howard, Mabel Lane, Ruth Latham, Margaret Marshall MacIlroy, Grace M. S. MacNeil, the late Annabelle Maxie, the Mazique family, Allie Minette Middleton, the late Katherine Grafton Miller, Mississippi Department of Archives and History, Mississippi University for Women, Frank Moran, George Moss, Natchez Garden Club, Natchez Historical Society, The Natchez Little Theatre, Natchez Pilgrimage Tours, Devereux Nobles, Suzannah Patterson, Shirley Petkovsek, Pilgrimage Garden Club, Ed Prince, Jane Prospere, Betty Ratcliffe, the late Danny Richardson, Earl M. Norman, Henry Norman, Lani Riches, Paul Schilling, Betty Jean Smith, Marion Smith, Thornton Smith, William E. Stewart, Mark Thompson, Elliott Trimble, Trinity Episcopal Church, Margaret Veller, certain anonymous collectors and collections in the public domain.

About the Authors . . .

DAVID G. SANSING, professor of history at The University of Mississippi, holds B.A. and M.A. degrees from Mississippi College, Clinton, and a Ph.D. degree from The University of Southern Mississippi, Hattiesburg. He is author of *Mississippi, 1540 to the Present; The Governor's Mansion, A Pictorial History*, with Alice McCardle and Charles McKeller; *A History of the Mississippi Governor's Mansion*, with Carroll Waller; *Mississippi: Its People and Culture; Mississippi Life: Past and Present*, with Ray Skates; *Mississippi History Through Four Centuries;* and *Making Haste Slowly: The Troubled History of Higher Education in Mississippi*. A frequent lecturer, he is past president of the Mississippi Historical Society.

SIM C. CALLON, a Natchez native, with his brother John Callon in 1961 formed Callon Petroleum Company of Natchez and subsequently served the organization as president and chairman of the board. Currently he is consultant to the company. An avid amateur photographer and historian, he has presented numerous original illustrated lectures on a variety of historical subjects concerning Natchez to national, regional, state and local groups and is co-author with Carolyn Vance Smith of *The Goat Castle Murder: A True Natchez Story That Shocked the World*. He is a member of the board of directors of the Historic Natchez Foundation, has been active for decades in the Natchez Historical Society and is past president of the Natchez Rotary Club.

CAROLYN VANCE SMITH, who holds a B.A. degree from Mississippi University for Women, Columbus, and an M.A. degree from Vanderbilt University, Nashville, Tennessee, is an award-winning educator who is coordinator of the English Department and director of public information at Copiah-Lincoln Community College in Natchez. She is author of hundreds of magazine and newspaper articles and numerous non-fiction books, all about Natchez. Founder of the Natchez Literary Celebration and a frequent lecturer, writing consultant and judge, she has held top leadership positions in the Natchez Historical Society, the Mississippi Historical Society and The Order of the First Families of Mississippi, Inc., and is past president of the national Mississippi University for Women Alumnae Association.

Index